Tail Gunner

A PATHFINDER'S WAR

A PATHFINDER'S WAR

AN EXTRAORDINARY TALE OF
SURVIVING OVER 100 BOMBER
OPERATIONS AGAINST ALL ODDS

Flight Lieutenant Ted Stocker DSO DFC C.Eng.

M.I.Mech.E. RAF Ret'd

with Sean Feast

GRUB STREET · LONDON

Published by
Grub Street Publishing
4 Rainham Close
London
SW11 6SS

British Library Cataloguing in Publication Data available on request

ISBN: 9781906502522

Typeset by Pearl Graphics, Hemel Hempstead

Printed and bound by MPG Ltd, Bodmin, Cornwall

Grub Street Publishing uses only FSC (Forest Stewardship Council) paper for its books

Contents

FOREWORD

The author is an ex-Halton aircraft apprentice, a body of RAF men of whom it is often said can 'go anywhere and do anything'. This is well borne out by *A Pathfinder's War*, which is really three books in one.

The first section relates how a farmer's boy aged 15 joins the Royal Air Force, trains for almost three years as a fitter, but then becomes a flight engineer in Bomber Command, flying first the Halifax and then Lancasters throughout the whole of the Second World War. Not only was Ted Stocker one of the very first men to wear the flight engineer's 'wings', but he went on to achieve the very rare distinction of winning the Distinguished Service Order (DSO) in those duties. He is also a remarkable survivor. As he mentions in the book, as early as 1943 only 2.5% of all aircrew lived to see the end of two flying tours, i.e. 50 operational missions. Ted was still going strong after no fewer than four tours and more than 100 operational sorties. As he tells us himself, he is a 'walking miracle'.

The five chapters dealing with his wartime experiences will be of particular interest to aviation historians, showing as they do the remarkable variation of operations that the Pathfinder force led all across Europe. The last part of the book is no less interesting for the variety of post-war flying in which he was involved, for example taking 'Bomber' Harris on a tour of Brazil at the end of the war, and then crewing the first of the new Neptune aircraft across from the United States when these aircraft came to equip Coastal Command. Even that did not complete his remarkable career, since he then left the RAF and went into industry, first with De Havilland and then into the petro-chemical industry – truly as colourful and as fulfilling a life as anyone could wish for.

Air Chief Marshal Sir Michael Armitage KCB CBE
Former Halton aircraft apprentice

PROLOGUE

In 1937 all aviation-mad youths such as myself knew that the revolutionary Mayo Composite aircraft was being built at Short Brothers works at Rochester, and my friend and I had a geographical advantage. We could cycle to the factory in an hour or less, and camp out at a public right of way between the hangar and the slipways. From there we could see the flying boats and seaplanes moored in the river only a dozen yards away.

The premise for Mayo was simple: tests had proven that an Imperial Airways' Empire flying-boat could achieve a transatlantic crossing only if its entire payload consisted of fuel. Since it was well known that an aircraft could be flown at a much greater weight than that at which it can take off from the ground, aircraft designer Robert Mayo proposed that a small heavily loaded mail-plane be carried to operational altitude above a larger 'mother plane' and then released to complete its long-range task. The proposal was accepted by the Air Ministry, and the aircraft manufacturer Shorts contracted to design and build the composite unit. The Short S21 Maia, the lower component, was a slightly enlarged and modified version of the Empire 'boat'; the Short S20 Mercury, the upper long-range unit, was an entirely new high-wing twin-float seaplane with four engines and a range of 3,800 miles.

The Maia first flew on July 27, 1937 and the Mercury 13 days later. We made several trips to see them on the river and on at least one occasion saw the pair perched on top of each other. At the controls of Maia was Captain A. Wilkinson; in command of Mercury was a young Australian, already a well-known name in aviation circles as a master navigator and 'airman extraordinary' in every sense. One day in the playground at school as I saw the full eight-engined Mayo Composite aircraft fly over, I could not possibly know that only a few years later I would be sat in the co-pilot's seat next to this very same man, the man who would become the pioneer and founder of the Pathfinder force, Donald Bennett.

CHAPTER ONE

LEARNING

Like hundreds of little boys before me, and many thousands since, I had always wanted to be a pilot. Born on August 31, 1922, just four years after the end of the First World War, aircraft fascinated me. I fed unashamedly on a diet of war books and aircraft manuals, and was a particular fan of W. E. Johns and his eponymous hero Biggles.

My love of flying was an escape from school where I enjoyed a steady, if unspectacular, career. I lost out on the lottery of state education. At junior school, initially, I did fairly well, usually finishing in the top three or four of my class, and occasionally first. Then the education authorities made a small change in the age groups and I found myself in a class with boys who had been at the school a year longer. Not surprisingly, when the eleven plus exam came along I was still struggling to catch up and failed. For this reason, and a fight with the headmaster's son, I was held down a year. The school was Sheerness Junior Technical School which had been built in 1910, and served as a hospital in the First World War. Among my contemporaries was a youngster called Norman Penney, whose uncle Bill Penney had also been a pupil there and had become Lord Penney of East Hendred OM KBE, the first director of British nuclear weapons research.

It was generally accepted when we were at school, and perhaps therefore a sign of the times, that university was reserved for grammar school boys, whereas the rest of us went to technical school. Our headmaster, Dr Bell, wanted to put Bill Penney up for university but was told by the Kent education authority that he 'was not university material'. Later when Bill became famous and his exploits were reported in the press at various times, 'Dinger' Bell (as our headmaster was inevitably nicknamed) would send the authorities the cuttings with a note stuck on the bottom that simply said 'not university material!'

Living so close to the sea, most of my friends found their careers already mapped out for them by their families, and this usually meant either an apprenticeship in His Majesty's dockyards, or joining the navy itself as an artificer apprentice. My father was a grazier who had lied about his age to sign up for the Boer War but was rejected for being too short. He volunteered again for the First World War and served in the trenches. He later ran sheep on a nearby rifle range as well as a small plot of land that we owned on the edge of Sheerness. My father had already warned me that a career in farming offered nothing but hard work and little reward, and was encouraging of my proposals to join the Royal Air Force, which I could do via an apprenticeship at RAF Halton.

There was one other boy at the school whose father was in the RAF at Eastchurch, and the pair of us decided we would sit the RAF entrance exams. I had talked to my cousin, an equipment officer, and he advised me to become an apprentice at Halton because in his words 'you could go anywhere from there, and do anything.' So I took his advice. Dinger Bell didn't want me to take the exam when I did – he wanted me to wait until the next summer and finish off my education properly – but I ignored him. That's why I was only 15 when I ended up in the air force.

I used to cycle up to Eastchurch for Empire Air Days and to Leysdown because there was an armaments range there and I would watch the aircraft dropping bombs on targets out to sea, but my knowledge of Halton was virtually nil. Fair to say I was soon to be much better informed.

RAF Halton had initially been home to 3 Squadron of the Royal Flying Corps, on an estate loaned to them by the local landowner Alfred Rothschild of international banking fame. With the outbreak of the First World War, the site became a major training ground for the army as it looked to recruit thousands of new volunteers and prepare them for the killing fields of the Western Front. As the camp expanded, temporary accommodation gave way to the erection of more permanent structures, and a major building programme began. At much the same time, the RFC was looking for a further facility for the training of air mechanics, having outgrown its Farnborough base. Halton was considered ideal, and so the building programme was accelerated to include new workshops, the physical work being completed by German prisoners of war.

By Armistice Day there were some 6,000 British and Australian male mechanics, 2,000 female mechanics and 2,000 boys being trained by some 1,700 staff. With peace came change. The Royal Air Force, as it had now become, needed permanent bases and having invested so much in Halton, negotiated to buy the entire estate to house its new No 1 School of Technical Training. With the negotiations successfully concluded, the RAF injected further funding to construct new barrack blocks, messes and an education block to replace the acres of wartime wooden huts. The narrow gauge railway link to Wendover station, which had been used to transport timber from the estate in support of the war effort, was replaced with a standard gauge branch line, to bring in coal and building materials.

Plans were laid for a permanent hospital, to replace the temporary wartime structure, and a headquarters formation moved into Halton House. As he re-organised the RAF to meet the requirements of peace, the 'father' of the RAF, Lord Trenchard, foresaw the need to produce a pool of skilled aircraft mechanics and Halton was selected as the home for the RAF aircraft apprentice scheme with its launch in 1920. Some 186 apprentice 'entries' would be trained between 1920 and 1993 and the training they received was to be thorough and broad-based. Apart from the basic syllabus, which combined the academic and practical disciplines, there was a tremendous emphasis on sport (Halton had no fewer than 56 sports pitches) – a policy that helped many top-class athletes and sportsmen to emerge.[1]

---

[1]Arguably the most famous was Don Finlay, who was to represent Great Britain in three Olympic Games, the last as team captain. He was a successful fighter pilot who later returned to Halton as chief instructor.

For the less physically inclined there was gliding, shooting and the preparation for expeditions such as the Nijmegen Marches. All could indulge their interests and talents in the Halton Society (and later the Cosford Society), which supported acting, debating, aero-modelling, wireless building, photography, philately, expeditions to the battlefields of Belgium and many other activities. Their most ambitious project was the design and construction of a light aircraft, which became a successful competitor in air races in 1927 and 1928. Also, each wing had a band – a pipe band, a brass band and a flutes and drums band – behind which it marched between its accommodation and workshops, the 'schools' or the airfield (each Entry also tended to have it own individual pipe bands). The high standards of drill instilled by this practice and the proximity of the capital ensured the apprentices' participation in many major public events, which enhanced the school's prestige and the boys' esprit-de-corps. Many of these 'Trenchard Brats' as we were known went on to achieve notable success and a considerable number rose to the higher ranks during their subsequent careers.

RAF Halton, potentially, was an intimidating prospect for any youngster, and I was still very young, but I took it all in my stride and was undaunted at being away from home for the first time. It was probably no different from going away to board. It wasn't a military environment, not entirely; it was more like a school, and we were all kids together. Yes some of our intake were older than me and had already been in civil employment, and we had the senior apprentices who were 17 or 18 bossing us around, but then you would have that at any school in the form of 'prefects'. I recall two boys in particular who turned up in short trousers, and their first ever pair of long trousers were their RAF uniforms.

My memory of Halton being 'more like a school' resonates with contemporary literature at that time. The education was based on the English public school system. John Buchan, author of *The 39 Steps*, wrote in *The Spectator* (and quoted in an Air Ministry pamphlet): 'The day may come when few families in Britain will not have a member connected in some capacity with the RAF, whose young men will return to civil life looking back upon their years of service with the pride with which men look back on Eton or Oxford, and which engineering or scientific firms will regard training in the Force as a primary recommendation for employment.'

Not surprisingly, given the opportunity that such an establishment offered, the entrance exam was especially stiff. I was confronted with a variety of different papers including a general paper (with English composition) that included having to write an essay within one hour on one of the following subjects: winter sports on snow and ice; street noises; an air display; labour saving devices in the home; and the leading features of your favourite newspaper. The second half of that particular paper involved having to answer a series of shorter discussion questions covering history, politics, geography, physics, and biology.

My results suggest that I was up to the challenge, and I attained sufficient marks (I came 402nd out of more than 800) to be invited to enlist formally, as stated in my official papers, as 'No 573288 boy service aircraft apprentice' for 12 years regular service (after the age of 18) on January 25, 1938 as part of Entry 37.

Not long into my training I was to suffer my first setback. Having been seen by the medical officer (MO) on my arrival and declared fit for general service, I was soon after taken ill suffering from headaches, dizziness and nausea. I had a temperature of well over 100 degrees Fahrenheit and was admitted to the sickbay for three days. Although discharged, I was almost immediately again re-admitted with much the same symptoms, but my temperature now going through the roof. With a rash and conjunctivitis, I was diagnosed as suffering from measles and placed in isolation. Soon after I was transferred from the Maitland Surgery at Halton to the Princess Mary RAF Hospital as I had nasty swellings to my face and forehead. It was pretty clear that something more serious was wrong with me and the doctors linked it back to the scarlet fever immunization I had been given only days before. All of us new boys had been given a cocktail of jabs on our arrival, and I had clearly come off second best. In the end I was to stay in hospital for over a month, and had to have an operation over my left eye to drain the swelling. I was finally discharged on April 13, and given 10 days leave to recover. Although declared fit, it was an illness that was to plague me for the remainder of my service career.

Before falling ill I had been designated a fitter II, working on both engines (E) and airframes (A). The aircraft, however, were becoming more sophisticated with hydraulics and complicated fuel systems and so it was decided to split the 'trade' between Es and As. Whatever part of the course we had been studying at the time this decision was taken determined which 'trade' we would follow, and I was lucky in that I had been training on engines. We weren't allowed to choose; we just did as we were told. I was quite satisfied. Instead of rigging bi-planes, I was getting to work on Gypsy Moth engines.

'Remustered' as a fitter II (E) on August 18, 1938, and now fully fit, I continued contentedly with my education. One task that every 'Brat' will remember was when one day we were given a piece of cast iron and a block of brass. The task was then to file the base (which was three inches square and an inch thick) and the cube such that the one inch cube would fit into the base whichever way it was turned. We started with a bastard file, the roughest of all of the files, and then gradually worked our way through medium files and then much finer files until we were using files filled with chalk to generate a polishing action on the cube.

We learned that iron and brass have different properties and react differently to filing. With all the other activities we only spent about one third of our working hours in the workshop and it therefore took about three months of jolly hard work to complete. Indeed my middle finger has never been the same since!

You couldn't take any short cuts; it was just damn hard work. The idea was that it would teach us the precision engineering skills we would need and an understanding of the tolerances we would have to work with in all areas of aircraft engineering. Indeed the tribute to all apprentices that passed through Halton and unveiled by HM the Queen in 1997 is in the design of our brass block.

Of course being engineers we had access to the very latest

tools: we had a broad range of instruments, from the bluntest of devices for hammering or drilling to the finest of precision tools that could measure the thickness of the thinnest stretches of metal or wire. We learned everything in both theory and practice, including advanced mathematics with calculus. It is fair to say that we were spared nothing.

My progress during this time was steady, rather than spectacular. In my annual report for my first year (to January 1939) my mathematics was deemed average, but I excelled in science. My drawing was described as disappointing (with the infamous words 'could do better') and although considered a hard worker in general studies, my work was untidy. In all other matters 'technical' I was considered average, albeit making steady progress, with the exception of sport where it was decided I should show more enthusiasm.

My time as an apprentice was not confined to Halton, however. Shortly after remustering, our 5(A) Wing was transferred to become 1 Wing at RAF Cosford, a new camp in the process of being built. Some 275 apprentices in all were transferred in a single group amid fears that Halton was too much in the firing line to be safe from enemy bombing raids. Originally designated an aircraft storage unit (ASU), Cosford was later earmarked as 2 Technical Training School to ease the pressure on the RAF's existing facilities not just at Halton, but also Uxbridge and Cranwell.[2]

Cosford was to all intents and purposes a 'new' camp that was still being built when we got there. Our accommodation was designed such that there were two rows of huts with a gap in-between, and in the gap were corridors leading to the ablution block that was shared between the two huts. As most of us were still very young, Cosford (and Halton for that matter) exercised a 'no smoking' rule for the under 18s. To get round that, we would sneak off to the toilet cubicles to have a crafty smoke. The NCOs, of course, were alive to this, but couldn't see who was smoking behind the doors. One day, they

---

[2]By the outbreak of World War Two, Cosford had 3,580 trainees consisting of apprentices in the trades of (fitter) engines, airframes, armourers, plus a significant number of flight mechanics and flight riggers. The apprentice element was ordered back to RAF Halton in March 1940.

organised a party of workmen to come in and chop about eight inches or so off the top of the doors. Now the screws weren't that good on the hinges, and it happened one night that somebody took off the door on the NCOs' cubicle, screwed an eight inch high fragment on each hinge, and in doing so created a 'door' with a large gap in the middle. On one of these pieces was chalked the words: 'NCOs only'! Not surprisingly the NCOs were furious, but they had underestimated the fact that as trainee engineers with our own tool kits, screwdrivers weren't difficult to get hold of.

Discipline at Cosford, like Halton, tended to be harsh but (invariably) fair. Each apprentice carried a permanent pass (at Cosford the pass had a red and green front to match our red and green checked cap bands), and each pass included details such as whether the student was allowed to 'walk out' up to five miles from the base, or whether he had his parents permission to smoke. The whole smoking lark came to be quite a giggle; NCOs always trying to catch us out, and we as little more than kids doing our best not to get caught. Some of us had pipes, and somebody bet one of my friends that he couldn't march from the mess to the workshops and keep his pipe lit all of the way. He did.

Being young, we were not averse to the occasional bout of high-jinks. Most of it was pretty harmless stuff, although we did perhaps go a little too far once with the barber, or 'Sweeney' as we called him after Sweeney Todd. Sweeney was a rather unpleasant fellow who was universally disliked. Military haircuts were all very well, but in our opinion he used to go a bit mad. Let's just say they were more army than air force. One night, he was just locking up when a hand went around the door and the light went off. A group of us went in, bound him in the chair, and shaved his head almost bald in a strip from the back of his head to the forehead with a pair of electric clippers. The authorities weren't very happy about it, but neither did they seem to be in too much of a hurry to find out who did it, which was probably just as well.

Our dentist, too, was the cause for much concern, although unlike the barber he commanded our utmost respect. His name was Cecil Beamish, an Irishman, and he came from a family of rugby-playing brothers and RAF-types who all made their mark in the forces. George Beamish became commandant of Cranwell in 1949 and retired as Air Marshal Sir George Beamish KCB, CB, CBE as C-in-C Technical Training Command; Charles retired as a group captain with the DFC in 1946; Victor was a famous Battle of Britain pilot and station commander at RAF Kenley, shot down and killed in 1942 as a group captain with the DSO & Bar, DFC and AFC; and then Cecil who went on to become director of RAF Dental Services and retire as an air vice-marshal CB in 1973. He was five times RAF golf champion and played rugby for the RAF and Ulster. George was capped 26 times for Ireland, and captained the team on four occasions. Charles won 12 caps. Victor, like Cecil, played for the RAF and Ulster, and later the Leicester Tigers, London Irish and Harlequins. He just missed out on an international cap. Such was the size of 'our' Beamish, that if he ever asked me to 'open wide', I always did as I was told.

The apprenticeship was meant to last three years, but the onset of war led to our course being truncated to two years and four months, primarily by removing sport and fitness from the syllabus. (Later, during the Battle of Britain, the course would be shortened further to one year and 10 months, and the newly-qualified youngsters could find themselves under attack within a few days of leaving their education. Indeed it was only by the time of the 43rd Entry that the full three-year term was re-instated. By a strange quirk, any of those under the age of 17 and a half were considered to be too young to fight in the war and – like me therefore – not eligible for the Defence Medal.)

September 3, 1939 is a day that we all remember, the day that war was finally declared. We were on church parade and the padre said that Chamberlain was on the radio so he was going to cut the service short, which was decent of him. We all ran over to the NAAFI because there was a big wireless set there that we could listen to (personal radios were a bit of a luxury in those days). After we heard the prime minister dolefully tell us that we were now at war with Germany, we all hung around discussing it. As you can imagine, it was all rather exciting.

By now it was about lunchtime so we went back to our huts to collect our 'irons' (as we called our cutlery) and on our way out again we were accosted by some snotty corporal physical training instructor (PTI) who demanded to know why we weren't all carrying our gas masks. 'Don't you know there's a war on?' he said, being very smug. Then he realised that it wasn't just a few of us that didn't have our gas masks, none of us did, and since he couldn't put us all on charge (we would have been there all day) he had to let us go.

As an aside, after Chamberlain came back from his meeting with Hitler in 1938 waving his piece of paper and declaring peace in our time, we were all issued with gas masks that were marked 'for drill purposes only'. It was only a year later when the war started for real that we were trusted with the real thing.

There were other changes too. At Halton we used to march in fours. Half-way though Cosford, however, everything changed to marching in threes. There was a very good reason for this that had been brought about by the start of the war. It had been found that when a squad marches in fours, if an aircraft came down to do some strafing, nobody knew which direction to run, and more of them were caught in the open; when there are threes, the two on the outside go to the outside ditches, and if the chap left in the middle in front of you went to the left, you went to the right. That way there was no panic to get into the trenches, and there were fewer casualties as a result.

Having survived the course, and not been subjected to testing Cosford's theory about marching in threes, I took my final exams in the winter of 1939/40, an exhaustive round of three-hour papers on science, aeronautical science, practical mathematics and mechanics, and the inevitable general studies. I passed, somewhere in the middle of the pack, and was able to celebrate my passing out as an apprentice with the sumptuous fayre of Mulligatawny soup followed by a choice of plaice or chicken, all washed down with a glass of lemonade! We were also able to enjoy the Cosford Society's final swansong, a revue evening entitled 'Bits and Pieces' granted by the kind permission of Cosford's commanding officer and First World

War air observer, Group Captain W. Budgen OBE. By the
seventh act, some wag had deigned to write on the programme
that it was still not too late to make it to the cinema if they
hurried.

Again my progress was monitored and reported in my
annual appraisal (December 1939) where it was apparent that
my concentration was waning. 'Could do better' is a phrase
that once again appears all too often, and my marks for testing
my practical and theoretical knowledge of things 'technical'
were unspectacular. I was told that I would have to work
harder if better results were to be achieved.

On March 13 I was again laid low by a bout of influenza
that put me out of action for 10 days, but having been finally
released from the station hospital I formally finished my
apprenticeship as an AC1 – an aircraftsman first class – on
March 23, 1940, one of a new generation of Brats with a
broad range of skills that would hopefully stand me in good
stead in the future. There were in fact three levels of passing
out. AC2, AC1 and LACs (leading aircraftsman), the latter in
my day being a bit thin on the ground. These were normally
the brightest or I used to think those who had managed to
achieve a good rapport with the disciplinarians on the base and
had been made corporal apprentice or sergeant apprentice
during training. Actually, it was those who got more than 80%
in their final test jobs, regardless of how well behaved they
might have been.

My cousin had suggested that as an apprentice, I could go
anywhere. As it was, my first posting turned out to be one of
the most serendipitous in what was to prove a long and
eventful career: the Aeroplane and Armament Experimental
Establishment (A&AEE) at Boscombe Down, Wiltshire.

*   *   *

The A&AEE, in its entirety, had only recently moved to
Boscombe Down from Martlesham Heath. The facility had
been established to test all new aircraft, systems and weaponry
then being trialled for use in the Royal Air Force. This included
not only those aircraft built by British manufacturers – A. V.
Roe, Handley Page, Short Brothers, Supermarine, Hawker et al

– but also those from overseas manufacturers – Bell, Curtiss and Brewster to name just a few. (It would also, later, become the facility for testing captured Axis aircraft.)

The diversity of aircraft confronting me as a new AC1 was both daunting and exciting in equal measure, for I found myself surrounded by a huge variety of aeroplanes from a lumbering old Vickers Virginia, a throwback to the First World War bi-plane era that had first flown in 1922, through to an early twin-engined Vickers Wellington with a clear canopy and gun but no turrets, and the colossal frame of the ultra-modern Short Stirling, then on the verge of entering service as Bomber Command's first four-engined 'heavy'.

I think I realised pretty quickly that I had fallen on my feet. Most of my contemporaries went to a squadron or a maintenance unit where they were dealing just with one type of aircraft, but at Boscombe Down we had every aircraft under the sun and you never knew what you were going to deal with next. We even had experimental types such as the Martin Baker fighter that was compared favourably to the Spitfire but never entered production or service, despite its promise.

The timing of my arrival coincided with one of the busiest and most exciting periods in aviation history. The 'Phoney' war soon gave way to the assault proper by the Germans in Belgium, Holland and into France. The Dutch surrendered in four days. By May 25, 1940 the British Expeditionary Force (BEF) was in full retreat, and the miracle of Dunkirk followed shortly after. French resistance crumbled, and the humiliation was complete. By June 25, it was all over, and Britain and its depleted armed forces stood alone behind white-chalk cliffs to await the inevitable invasion. Whenever we went into Salisbury, where many of the army survivors were recovering, our uniforms prompted the question 'where was the RAF?' – and it was a question that was never politely put.

One of the first things I learned at this new posting, apart from how to change the gearbox of a tractor, was how to drive. After Dunkirk, of course, the RAF lost a large proportion of its motor transport (MT) fitters and indeed whole sections in France, and that is why I suddenly found myself behind the wheel. Each Flight had to send a fitter to the MT yard for a month. I could ride a bike (I had a BSA 150 motorbike – the then love of my life) but had never driven a car, let alone a lorry, and didn't have a license, but when our Chiefy told me to get on with moving lorries around the yard I just got on with it! One of the vehicles was a 1917 Leyland petrol bowser that was older than me, and I had to drive it every time an aircraft needing refuelling. It had the usual three pedals, and two levers, one was a manual throttle and the other a lever with 'advance' and 'retard' on the steering column. You moved another lever, engaged the clutch and the pump was working. (Later, when I was on 35 Squadron, one of the girls who drove the crew buses was encouraged or dared to get this vehicle as close to the Halifax as she could. And she did. She managed to get the thing stuck between the tail unit and the mainplane! She was in a bit of a flap so I got it out for her. All that training wasn't wasted I suppose.)

Britain's land forces may have been temporarily defeated but the fight was far from finished. The Air Ministry rapidly accelerated the development of new and ever more innovative aircraft on which it pinned its hopes for the future, however black it seemed. Within weeks of my arrival, the second prototype (designated K7605) of the Short S.29 Stirling with its powerful Bristol Hercules engines and distinctive landing gear and twin tail wheels arrived at Boscombe for service tests and trials. (The first prototype had been damaged so badly on landing as to be effectively written off.) Main production had already started, whilst the aircraft was still officially being put through its paces.

In September, the second prototype (L7245) of the Handley Page HP57, later known as the Halifax, also arrived at Boscombe to join the original prototype (L7244) for an extensive series of tests. (In July 1941, L7244 appears in my log book at 35 Squadron.) The second evolution was more representative of the final production series, being fitted with mock ups of the nose and tail power-operated gun turrets and two floor guns situated in the fuselage well position aft of the bomb bay. The following month, the first production model (L9485) also arrived to join the test programme, distinguishable primarily, I noticed, by its beam gun hatches. With my engineer's eye, I also noticed the change from the De Havilland three-bladed metal propellers to Rotol constant speed units with compressed wooden blades.

The diversity of the aircraft was matched only by the diversity of the characters that tested them. Two of the more senior officers were 'Sludge' Collings and Albert Groom. Raymond Collings, also known as 'Fatty' for largely obvious reasons, was a pre-war regular, who had joined the RAF in the mid-1920s. By the time I first met his acquaintance, he was a well-respected test pilot with A Flight, Performance Testing Squadron (A&AEE). On November 5, 1940, with the resurrection of 35 Squadron attached to the A&AEE, Collings took command of what was to become the first Halifax-equipped squadron of Bomber Command.

Wing Commander Albert Groom MBE AFC DSM, meanwhile, was the establishment's bombing expert. A veteran of the First World War, with his Distinguished Service Medal (DSM) denoting his one-time non-commissioned status, Groom had been posted to Boscombe Down in September 1939 and was officer commanding the unit's armament division. Nearby Porton Down had two enormous concrete blocks, twice as high as a hangar and about half as wide, that they used as a bombing 'target'. Groom would be regularly seen droning over the target in the old Virginia testing the latest bombsights.

Probably one of the most remarkable characters that I came across was Stanley Watts, a First World War balloonatic and post-war member of Alan Cobham's Flying Circus. Stanley Langford Conway Watts to give him his full name and handle, but known universally as 'Pop', had joined the Royal Naval Air Service (RNAS) – a forerunner to the RAF – in 1916, transferring to the Royal Air Force in April 1918.

At the beginning of 1941, Pop was awarded the Air Force Medal (AFM), a rare accolade given to NCO aircrew (the officer equivalent was the Air Force Cross – the AFC) for outstanding feats of airmanship whilst not in action with the enemy. The AFM and Great War service medals beneath his flight engineer brevet marked Pop down as something of a legend.

Another great character and outstanding test pilot with whom I flew on a number of occasions (usually in the Stirling as a nominal flight engineer) was John Dutton, a 30-year-old from Rotherham. Dutton, a flight commander, was also to be given the AFC, awarded to him in the same New Year's honours list as Pop Watts' AFM. He had only recently been promoted squadron leader when he was detailed on March 1, 1941 to test a new Curtiss Mohawk.

The Mohawk (the Curtiss-Wright Corporation H75 'Hawk' but operating in the RAF as the P-36 Mohawk) was a radial-engined single-seat fighter built in the US and originally destined for the French Armée de l'Air as a 'stop-gap' solution in the late 1930s when the French suddenly realised they had insufficient modern aircraft to protect themselves from aerial attack. Too little too late they decided upon the Hawk, then in plentiful supply. It was a Hawk, indeed, that actually shot down the first Luftwaffe aircraft during the Battle of France and the aircraft accounted for more Germans than any of the home-grown Morane Saulnier or Dewoitine fighters, excellent though they were.

With the surrender of France some pilots flew their aircraft to Britain although more sided with the Vichy government in the south of France. The remaining French Hawks were shipped directly to Britain, still in French camouflage and with French instruments and equipment installed. It was one such aircraft, Serial No BK877 (the 99th A-4 model, which had been completed in May 1940), that Dutton was instructed to fly in order to test the heating equipment for the aircraft's six Browning machine guns as they had a tendency to freeze when above 20,000ft.

The aircraft, in its bright yellow colour-scheme to easily distinguish it as a new/experimental 'type' and avoid incidents with friendly fire, took off without any difficulty shortly after 10:00 a.m. At 10:30 a.m. the Mohawk was seen to dive, burning, out of the cloud base and bury itself in a large crater. Test pilots would always try to bring an aircraft back for analysis rather than abandon it and lose the results of their work. Perhaps Squadron Leader Dutton was killed trying to bring his burning aircraft back to base. I had been a fitter on the Mohawk, and remember the crash, but my memory differs as regards whether the aircraft was on fire as some suggest when it fell to earth. A witness I spoke to said the plane went straight in, with no mention of fire. I saw no sign of burning on any part of the plane we recovered, and there were no signs in the surrounding area to indicate that the pilot had attempted a false landing.

What I certainly remember, is the grim task of trying to recover the body, for I was one of the party sent out to bring what was left of the aircraft back. It was sunken into a marshy area, a bit like a pond. We had a river anchor with two hooks and sent that down attached to a winch on the bowser to dredge what was there. We got most of the aircraft up and most of him. It wasn't a very pleasant job, and one of the senior NCOs watching collapsed at the sight.

I remember speaking to Dutton's wife after the war at the station commander's house (Group Captain Ronnie Lees) at Bassingbourn; I did not mention the fact that I was the engine fitter on her husband's plane or on the party recovering her husband's body. I thought that would be too distressing.

I also remember that particular aircraft for a different reason, because it was how I learned to change a propeller in rapid time. A Mohawk used six brownings in all, four in the wings, and two that fired through the prop, like something out of the First World War, but these didn't seem to work very well. The ammunition you used needed to be top quality; it was not unusual that within a belt of ammunition, you occasionally got a 'slow' bullet. Trouble is, when that happens it simply smashes into the prop, damaging the metal blades and causing an imbalance. I changed many propellers on that aircraft!"[3]

Dutton's death came towards the end of my time at Boscombe. For many months prior to the incident, I had been working the system, trying to achieve my real ambition of becoming a pilot. But there was a problem. To be accepted for pilot's training required a minimum rank of leading aircraftsman (LAC) and I was still only an AC1. To get to LAC

---

[3]The Mohawk was tested at Boscombe Down against a Spitfire and as a result the type was deemed unfit for service in Europe and the remaining aircraft were shipped to Asia to fight the Japanese.

and therefore apply for a pilot's course I had to do a trade test. There was a corporal there, a pre-war regular, an Ulsterman as old as the hills (he was probably in his 30s or something). He had taken 12 years to get from LAC to corporal, and had been on one unit with Lawrence of Arabia (or Shaw as I think he liked to call himself then to protect his anonymity). He was very good to me, and helped me with what I was likely to be asked. He also helped me with the test piece so that I was well prepared.

Of course the day came for the test and I passed it without too much difficulty. The only problem was, I did a little too well, because four months later I'd been promoted temporary corporal and then was considered too senior to be allowed to leave! All was not totally lost, however. At about the same time an Air Ministry order was posted to say that they were looking for sergeants, corporals, or exceptional LACs, all had to be fitters of course, for the role of flight engineers. I thought that if I couldn't be a pilot, then I might just as well be a flight engineer. Having put my name down I found I was on the train within a couple of weeks, which for the air force was pretty quick going.

I soon discovered that flight engineer was a new 'trade' brought about by the increasing sophistication of the aircraft coming into service. The twin-engined Whitley and Wellington, now denoted as 'medium bombers' were steadily giving way to the 'heavies' – the Stirling and Halifax (and later the Lancaster) with ever more complex systems and technology. The pilot alone could not possibly keep watch on the dials for each of the four engines as well as his own flying instruments and keep the aircraft in the air all at the same time, and was in no position to monitor such detail as fuel efficiency, engine temperatures, coolant levels etc. that could make all the difference between flying or crashing. An obvious solution was for a new member of the crew to handle these increased responsibilities, and so the idea of the flight engineer was born.

Training at this stage of the war was minimal yet this was understandable given that nearly all of the first generation of flight engineers were similar to me in that they had effectively already been 'trained' on the job. What they weren't trained for, however, and an area that nearly all 'trades' at that time had to be skilled in, was air gunnery. God knows why we had to do air gunnery to be a flight engineer but we did. There were 12 of us on the course: 10 are dead, one's blind and then there's me. Survival was the name of the game. You stayed alive you got the gongs.

Anyhow I soon found myself posted to No 8 Bombing & Gunnery School in Evanton, the other side of Inverness, arriving at the tiny railway station beside the Cromarty Firth on May 5, 1941, a short march from the base. The course itself was mercifully short, only three weeks. For weaponry, I was trained on the eponymous Browning .303 machine guns (I don't think I got to look at the Vickers 'K' which was the other standard armament at that time). For aircraft, the school used one of the RAF's first monoplane bombers, the Handley Page Harrow. The first Harrows had entered service with 214 Squadron in 1937, and by the outbreak of war, Harrows and Whitleys were the two principal heavy bombers the service could muster. In the event, the Harrow was not employed in a heavy bomber capacity, and was relegated to transport duties, a role, ironically, for which it had originally been designed. (In September 1944, two 271 Squadron Harrows evacuated wounded troops from the ill-fated Arnhem operation.)

The Harrow had few vices. Powered by two 925hp Bristol Pegasus XX engines, she cruised at around 163mph at 15,000ft, and could break the 200mph barrier if pushed. For armament she had four .303 Brownings mounted in the nose, dorsal and tail power-operated turrets. It was an ideal training platform.

I took my first flight on the morning of May 12, 1941, in Harrow K6978 skippered by a Flight Lieutenant Leslie. I spent an hour in the air, shooting at a target at sea. I was up again later that afternoon with Sergeant Piwko (in Harrow K6982), conducting beam attacks on a drogue. The next 10 days followed a similar pattern, nearly always with a different pilot and rarely in the same aircraft. On May 19, an early morning sortie with Pilot Officer Ryteer had to be abandoned because of bad weather; three hours later I took off with Squadron Leader Suryn only to have my weaponry malfunction; a third attempt with Sergeant Farthing had to be aborted when the turret jammed.

Despite these minor setbacks, I finally managed to satisfy the examiners in all of the necessary tests: on the ground at 200 yards, and in the air firing air-to-ground, beam, beam RS, and free astern without harming myself or probably more importantly, anyone else. In total I spent more than 13 hours in the air, achieving an examination mark of 66%. On my record showing the results of my ab initio gunnery course, the officer commanding (Wing Commander Slater) has written: 'Keen and interested. Wants more practice on gun handling.' It is not recorded whether 'wants' should read 'needs'!

The course ended on May 24, 1941, and the very next day I was posted to 76 Squadron at Linton-on-Ouse. But there was a hitch: 76 Squadron did not seem to have any aircraft. The problem was rectified in true service style. I was posted the next day to a squadron that did have aircraft, 35 Squadron, the first to operate the new Halifax.

CHAPTER TWO

OPERATING

35 Squadron was originally formed as part of the Royal Flying Corps on February 1, 1916, taking part in the battles of Arras, The Somme, Ypres and Cambrai. Disbanded in 1919, it was reformed 10 years later as a bomber squadron and saw action in the Sudan following the Italian invasion of Abyssinia. The squadron returned to the UK in 1936, and became part of the newly-formed Bomber Command and given its own squadron crest and motto: uno animo agimus – we act with one accord.

With the outbreak of the Second World War, the squadron had become part of 6 Group based at Cranfield and began equipping with Blenheim twin-engined fighter/bombers soon after. Within a handful of weeks the squadron became part of 4 Group and was earmarked to receive the first production Halifax Mk I bombers. The squadron at this time comprised only five pilots in all, including the commanding officer and a man with whom I was already acquainted, Wing Commander 'Fatty' Collings.

Collings took the squadron to Linton-on-Ouse on December 12, 1940 where conversion and training flights continued apace as more of the new bombers arrived. 'Pop' Watts had also arrived to assist with the conversion as a senior flight engineer, then tasked with bringing the newest generation of 'trade' up to speed with their particular 'type'.

I was to fly three different series of the Mk I Halifax whilst with 35 Squadron. The Mk I had a 22ft bomb bay as well as six bomb cells in the wings, enabling it to carry 13,000lb (5,897kg) of bombs. Defensive armament consisted of two .303 Browning machine guns in the nose and four in a tail turret; the early aircraft also had a pair of VGOs (Vickers Gas

Operated) at each waist position, although these would soon be removed. We operated with a crew of six: two pilots, a navigator, a flight engineer, a wireless operator and one gunner. In action, the wireless operator and flight engineer were to man the waist guns and indeed did so on some of the earlier daylight raids. The first batch of Mk I Halifaxes were designated Mk I Series I; the Mk I Series II increased the aircraft's gross weight (from 58,000lb to 60,000lb) and the Mk I Series III increased fuel capacity.

The performance of the Mk I was impressive: it was powered by four 1,130hp Rolls-Royce Merlin X engines that gave her a top speed of 255mph at 7,000ft, and a cruising speed of a little under 200mph at 15,000ft. Its service ceiling was 18,000ft – high enough to avoid the light flak, but still comfortably in range of heavier artillery. Its biggest problem, and one that perhaps they never really solved, was its weight, and of course its rudders. Whilst it was being tested at the A&AEE, its all-up weight, originally designed not to exceed 18 tons, had in fact exceeded 24, and was close to 25. The twin rudders had proved inadequate in keeping the aircraft straight on take-off, and there was a tendency for them to overbalance at low airspeeds, when making tight turns, or if a propeller was feathered. They were especially unresponsive at speeds below 120mph – a serious shortcoming that was to have far-reaching consequences on its operational performance and development.

From an engineer's perspective, the Halifax was also not without its foibles, especially in terms of its hydraulics. Most hydraulics systems worked on a pump that via a valve allowed high-pressure oil to flow on one side of the piston in a hydraulic jack, whilst oil from the other side could flow back to the reservoir. If the pump of the engine driving it failed, then the jack could not be moved: if the undercarriage was up, it stayed up. Not on the Halifax. It had the French Messier system. Designed as what is now called 'a fail-safe system', the pump supplied high pressure to the side of the jacks that raised the wheels, raised the flaps and closed the bomb doors. The oil on the other side of each jack piston was in a sealed unit; oil was forced out into a sealed container that was part-filled with compressed air. This meant that the wheels could only be retracted and stay retracted as long as the pump and the engine driving it were working and keeping the air compressed. In an emergency the undercarriage could be lowered as the compressed air forced the oil back into the jack. Needless to say the system gave us quite a bit trouble before simple modifications were made, and being made in Paris, spares were also a little thin on the ground.

The 'trouble' cannot be understated. The main pipeline was known to burst. This meant that the bomb doors would open and the undercarriage would drop down, seriously impacting the flying characteristics of the aircraft. If you were over enemy territory when it happened, or under attack, it could kill you. The fluid used tended to have a low flashpoint, and on one occasion exploded and blew a large hole in the wing. All of these initial teething difficulties were ultimately overcome, but caused considerable consternation and frustration amongst the early Halifax crews. They later fitted a stopcock at the outlet from the hydraulic accumulators for the flaps and bomb doors, operated by the flight engineer. It wasn't possible for the undercarriage, so instead they fitted a large hook mechanism again operated from inside the aircraft that was also my responsibility.

By the time I arrived at Linton, the squadron had once again become operational, flying its first Halifax sortie (and indeed the first Halifax operation of the war) on March 10/11 1941 against Le Havre and Boulogne. Seven aircraft led by Wing Commander Collings were detailed for the attack, one of which, predictably, had to abort because of hydraulics trouble. Of the six others, Squadron Leader Peter Gilchrist DFC, the B Flight commander, had the most eventful night.

Having successfully bombed the docks and ridden through heavy flak, Gilchrist had just handed control over to his co-pilot and crossed the English coast when they came under attack from a nightfighter. Canon shells smashed into the instrument panel and the starboard outer was holed. Worse still, Ron Aedy, Gilchrist's flight engineer was hit and wounded in the knee. As quickly as he could, and suspecting that they were under attack from a British fighter and not a German one,

Gilchrist fired off the colours of the day, but by then the damage had been done. Believing the crew to have baled out, Gilchrist left the aircraft (L9489) himself, and the aircraft crashed not far from Guildford, the victim – as he had supposed – of one of the RAF's newest Boston nightfighters from 23 Squadron, RAF Ford. Sadly, as it happened, four of the crew had in fact not baled out, and died in the crash. Only Ron Aedy, the wounded flight engineer, survived, along with his skipper.

To me, life on an operational squadron was all very new and exciting. I was still only a temporary corporal, but I was happy with my posting, and Linton in particular. Linton was not far from York, and had been opened in 1937 as the headquarters of 4 Group. Interestingly at that time the AOC 4 Group was Arthur Harris who would later, of course, take charge of Bomber Command. Being a permanent base, it was quite luxurious – certainly in relation to other airfields on which I served later in the war. The facilities were excellent.

The facilities at the base were surpassed only by the building requisitioned by the RAF for the aircrew mess, known as Beninbrough Hall. Beninbrough Hall had been built on the grounds of a former Elizabethan manor house in the early 18th century, and until 1827 was in the hands of the Bourchier family. With the sale of the estate in 1916 it was feared that the hall would be demolished, until a wealthy benefactor, Lady Chesterfield, stepped in and bought it, and set about its renovation. It was a magnificent red brick house, and although most of the expensive furnishings for which it was famed had of course been removed by the time we arrived, it was nonetheless pretty luxurious and set in the most beautiful grounds. The house was near a river that had its own ferry. Whenever we wanted to go to the pub we used to ring the hand-bell at the riverside for the ferry and over we went. If the bar wasn't staffed then we would pour ourselves a drink and put the money in the till. The pub had a radiogram but only one record – 'One fine day' by Judy Garland. It got a bit monotonous after a while.

In some awe of my new surroundings, I was also similarly impressed with my new squadron colleagues, and for very good reason. There were three officers on the flight I joined: Flight Lieutenant Leonard Cheshire; Flying Officer Peter Cribb; and Pilot Officer Edmund 'Keith' Cresswell. Cheshire needs no introduction, and both Peter Cribb (with whom I was to become particularly friendly) and Keith Cresswell went on to become two of the most famous Pathfinders in 8 Group later in the war, winning a chest full of medals between them.

I remember Cheshire getting his scraper ring (a 'half' ring to denote his promotion from flight lieutenant to squadron leader) and going off on a tour of America. His brother (Christopher) was also a pilot, with 76 Squadron, and was shot down quite early on. Paddy O'Kane was his flight engineer, another ex-apprentice, and his main job in life seemed to be looking after the Bentley motorcar that Cheshire had brought with him to Linton.

Cheshire had a DSO very early on whilst with 102 Squadron and he earned it for bringing back a Whitley that was severely damaged. He was very lucky to get away with it when you see the damage they inflicted on his aircraft. Attacking the railway yards at Cologne on the night of November 12/13, 1940, an anti-aircraft round passed through the front turret and exploded, blinding the pilot momentarily. Another shell burst behind the port wing, setting off a flare that exploded with incredible force, tearing a 10ft panel from the fuselage and severely burning the wireless operator in the face. Despite the shock, and the panel flapping in the slipstream, Cheshire managed to fly the crippled bomber back to base, where his actions were immediately recognised with the award of a DSO – an extremely unusual occurrence for an officer of such (then) junior rank.

Whilst the squadron was flying on operations, I was still very much being 'trained'. Supplementary courses, some lasting several weeks, were held for all novice flight engineers at Rolls-Royce in Derby to learn more about the latest Merlin engine variant, and at Handley Page at Cricklewood and Radlett for further instruction on airframes and hydraulics. I also had more practical 'hands-on' tuition flying with some of the squadron's more experienced pilots, among them Sergeant Stan Greaves.

Greaves was the first pilot with whom I flew in a Halifax, my log book describing me as a u/t engineer. I remember little about the flight beyond what I recorded at the time: 'July 23, 1941. Halifax I (Series I) L9512. Take off 16:35. A navigation training flight lasting 25 minutes.' What is perhaps more significant, is that Stan Greaves went missing from operations the next day.

Shortly after we landed, several of the crews were summoned to the briefing room at Linton, and told that they would be taking off almost immediately fully fuelled and with a full bomb load and flying to Stanton Harcourt in Berkshire from where they would be taking part in operations the next day. Intelligence reports had revealed that the German battle cruiser *Scharnhorst* had sailed from Brest to La Pallice near La Rochelle, and presented a grave threat to Allied shipping. This threat was heightened with news that a convoy with some 30,000 Canadian troops was currently on its way across the Atlantic to the UK. Nine aircraft from 35 Squadron and six from 76 Squadron were detailed to take out the *Scharnhorst* 'at all costs'.

At this stage in the war, there were many who thought that the heavy bombers had sufficient defensive armament to withstand fighter attack, even in daylight. Friendly escort was anyway out of the question, since no Allied fighters had the necessary range to make the 600-mile round trip. The result was a disaster waiting to happen, and it happened in spectacular style.

The aircraft flew at 1,000ft to avoid German radar but were spotted by a German destroyer still some 100 miles short of the target. It meant that when our chaps arrived, there were more than 30 German fighters waiting for them, as well as all of the flak that they had to contend with from the shore batteries and the guns from the *Scharnhorst* itself. It was a miracle any of them got home alive.

The cost to 35 Squadron was high. Flight Sergeant Clarence Godwin (L9527) was shot down and killed, only two of his crew making it out to survive as prisoners of war; Warrant Officer George Holden (later to become commanding officer of

617 Squadron) lost his rear gunner, Pilot Officer Harold Stone DFM, and two other crew members were wounded; four members of Squadron Leader Terrence Bradley's crew were wounded, one of them – Sergeant Peter Bolton – fatally; and Sergeant Walker in Pilot Officer Miller's crew was also hit in the leg, but survived. The only other aircraft shot down was the one piloted by Stan Greaves.

Greaves had been attacked even before he reached the target. A flak burst put one engine out of action and he was forced to abort his bombing run. Coming round again he was hit by flak in the fuselage and then the fighters struck. Greaves gave the order to bale out and I believe it took nearly 20 seconds for them all to get out of the aircraft before it exploded.

It was indeed a miracle that anyone got out of Halifax L9512 – the same aircraft in which I had flown the air test the day before. The bomb aimer, Sammy Walters, stayed with the aircraft just long enough to toggle away his bombs and managed to score a direct hit on the stern of the *Scharnhorst*. By the time Stan Greaves, as the last to go, took to his 'chute, they were down to one engine and had no fewer than seven Messerschmitt 109s queuing up to take pot shots at them.[4]

Despite the casualties (76 Squadron also lost three whole crews in the raid), the attack on La Pallice was by no means a failure. Although not mortally hit, the *Scharnhorst* was sufficiently damaged in the stern and the bridge that it had to return to Brest where it could be repaired in relative safety. The Canadian troop convoy, from the *Scharnhorst* at least, was no longer under any threat.

Few of the crews made it back to base, most landing wherever they could at airfields scattered across the southern counties. The following afternoon, I flew with Pilot Officer Jack McGregor-Cheers in the prototype Halifax L7244 to Weston Zoyland with the squadron engineering officer to pick up one of the crews and then on to the Coastal Command station at St Eval. Whilst on the ground at St Eval, where there had been an air raid the previous evening, I noticed a hydraulic

---

[4]After returning from Germany at the end of the war, Greaves was awarded a well-deserved DFM for his gallantry that day, and his bomb aimer was mentioned in despatches.

oil leak at the pump outlet. The fitting should have been replaced, but as these were made in Paris (I had said that spares were hard to come by) there was no chance of finding one in Cornwall. Not wishing to give the Luftwaffe an additional target if they returned, I visited the NAAFI and bought a large packet of chewing gum. I then went over to the engineering section to obtain rolls of insulating tape and copper wire. Back at the aircraft, I handed out the gum and told the rest of the crew to get chewing, but that I wanted it back when they'd finished. I wrapped the chewing gum around the leak, and used the insulating tape to hold the gum in place whilst I bound the copper wire around it to hold the pressure. It worked. We returned safely to Linton. I did not tell my squadron engineering officer, but I did tell the unfortunate fitter who would have to clean up the mess.

By July 27, all of the men that had made it back to the UK were either safely in Linton, or in various hospitals recovering from their wounds. This was probably the first time I actually stopped and thought about the danger of operations. Seeing the crews that made it back, their faces belied the horrors they had witnessed, and the terror they must have felt. Confident, highly-trained young men had been sorely tested in battle, and were badly shaken by the experience. I used to joke with some of the others that if I didn't make it back, they could have my prized sheepskin Irving flying jacket and vice versa. By the time I had collected three such jackets from aircrew who had failed to return, it ceased being so funny.

What also challenged my sense of humour was a 48-hour pass that I chose to spend in London with some friends. We decided to meet up at an expensive restaurant in Soho, and there I was, minding my own business, when two service police (SP) corporals came in and challenged me. I had my two stripes and an air gunner's badge that they told me I had no right to wear. 'You can't be a corporal air gunner, you'd be a sergeant' they said, and told me to take the badge off. I refused, and possibly made matters worse by telling them that I wasn't an air gunner, I was a flight engineer. Of course they'd never heard of such a trade, and decided to take me to their local station to verify my story. Again they told me to remove my brevet, and again I refused, so it became a stand-off. At last I suggested they called 35 Squadron and asked for the adjutant which they duly did. The adjutant was happy to tell them that not only did they have one corporal flight engineer, but actually they had several, and could they have me back! I was then unceremoniously thrown out of the cell and into the London blackout, and obliged to find my own way home.

After the excitement of La Pallice, I was keen to find myself a regular crew and begin operations, but spent a frustrating three months with neither looking a possibility. Meanwhile, however, life – and death – within the squadron continued. On August 14, Flying Officer Ronald Lisle and his crew were shot down attacking Magdeburg. There were no survivors. Two further aircraft were lost in August, including one piloted by Jack McGregor-Cheers. McGregor-Cheers, a likeable 24-year-old from Bradford, had gambled with death once before, having survived earlier in the month after being hit by flak and losing an engine over Berlin. In the crash landing that resulted, both pilot and second pilot were thrown out of the aircraft, the latter sustaining a broken ankle. In the event, it saved his life, for he was not flying the night that Jack went missing, never to return.

The losses continued to mount throughout September. Two crews were lost on the night of September 2/3: 28-year-old Flying Officer Ross James DFC (Halifax L9508) and Pilot Officer Douglas Fraser (L9560). Fraser, the son of a wing commander, was only 19 years old. On September 10/11, Flying Officer Williams' navigator mistook Cherbourg for the UK on their way back from Torino, and they all ended up 'in the bag' as a result. Five days later, 21-year-old Pilot Officer Harold Brown was killed when his Halifax went missing over Hamburg. The rest of his crew survived to become prisoners of war.

During this period, I flew whenever I could to increase my flying hours including two trips with Flight Lieutenant Cheshire in a modified Halifax I (Series III). My luck was to change, however, on October 4, when I was at last asked to crew up with my first 'permanent' skipper – a small Welsh dynamo by the name of Sergeant Williams.

I had only met Williams on a couple of occasions but was very friendly with his navigator who happened to be a rather good table tennis player, as was his wife, at a national level. Anyhow, the pace of training was now accelerating towards becoming fully operational. We flew three times on the 4th, testing the fuel consumption of our aircraft (a Series II), testing our gunners' response to fighter attacks, and our pilot's ability to fly in formation. By October 11 we were ready, and briefed to attack Essen in the Ruhr Valley.

Essen was one of Germany's 'vital centres' listed by the Air Ministry in a report published early in the war. It had identified that the nearest targets for its heavy bombers, apart from the north-western ports, were in the Rhineland, including the tremendous industrial concentration in the Ruhr. The Ruhr, approximately 300 miles from England in a straight line, was by far the most important industrial target in Europe, producing enormous quantities of steel, coal and metallurgical coke every month that made UK efforts look paltry by comparison. The two largest engineering firms in Europe at that time were also in the Ruhr, in Essen and Düsseldorf, with both cities featuring highly in the list of desirable targets:

City	Population	Industries
Essen	670,000	Krupps steel works
Duisberg	440,000	Transport, coal, steel
Bochum	634,000	Coal and iron
Düsseldorf	530,000	Transport, steel
Dortmund	550,000	Transport, steel, coke
Wuppertal	411,000	Chemicals
Krefeld	170,000	Steel works
Gelsenkirchen	323,000	Gas, coke, hydrogenation plant
München Gladbach	130,000	Textiles
Solingen	150,000	Steel works
Bottrop	86,000	Rheinische Stahlwerke

Ironically, the focus of Germany's might in one relatively compact area was also one of its biggest weaknesses. Imagine an area the size of London with engineering works, chemical plants, blast furnaces and coal mines all densely packed together and you have some idea of the concentration in the Ruhr Valley. This concentration, and the intricate nature of its supporting transport network and infrastructure, made the Ruhr an easy choice of target.

Essen in particular, although famous, had not yet become infamous in the minds of Bomber Command aircrew. I wasn't scared as such about going to Essen, but rather a little impatient. I felt I had been quite ready to go for some time; the fact that I was on operations was all that mattered. I remember the briefing very well, because I found it all so overwhelming trying to catch what everyone was saying as the CO, intelligence officer, met officer and various other specialists took it in turn to say their piece. It didn't take me too long to get used to it all, but at the time it was a bit of an eye opener.

As it happened, the attack on Essen on the night of October 10/11 was somewhat of a damp squib in the annals of Bomber Command. The days of the thousand bomber raids were still some way off, and only 78 bombers – a mixed bag of twin-engined Whitley and Hampden and four-engined Halifax bombers – were briefed for operations. Of those 78, one Whitley from 58 Squadron was lost to a nightfighter and another ran out of fuel, two Whitleys from 78 Squadron collided on take-off, and two Hampdens (one each from 83 Squadron and 106 Squadron) were shot down. Only 13 aircraft in all claimed to have bombed 'in the Essen area' because of bad weather. One aircraft from 35 Squadron (L9504) was damaged, and the pilot (Pilot Officer Norman) was lucky to land without further mishap. It was an inauspicious start.

My own abiding memory of the raid, my first trip, was that I could see nothing on the way out, and nothing on the way back. I looked out into the dark and remember thinking quite clearly: 'how the hell did we end up here?' It was chaotic, haphazard even, and I felt completely and utterly lost. We stooged around the night sky for what seemed an eternity and then all of a sudden I was aware that we were over the target and the pilot and the navigator were discussing where they should drop their bombs. They seemed to know what they were doing, even if I didn't, but I'm not convinced. But this was not unusual for bomber operations at that time. Until the end of 1941, bomber crews tended to operate individually rather than as part of a 'stream'. That would come later. For now we found our own way to the target and bombed when we got there. We could choose our own speed and height, the result being that attacks could be spread over several hours rather than concentrated into 20 minutes. One of the fears, so I understand, was collisions if too many aircraft were in the air in one place at roughly the same time. I believe experiments later proved this fear to be ungrounded.

There may have been good reason why I struggled to see anything of the target. Essen was in fact incredibly difficult to locate by night, certainly in the early years before the introduction of more sophisticated electronic aids. However, a further difficulty resulted from the industrial smoke emanating from the hundreds of chimneys that tended to form a blanket of smog through which little could be seen, so perhaps on reflection it wasn't quite as chaotic as I'd first imagined.

My second operation with Sergeant Williams, still in L9579, was as exciting as my first was uneventful, and nearly ended in disaster.

It is important to remember that the Halifax was originally designed as a relatively short-range bomber, and after Dunkirk there were some major modifications to ensure we could reach targets in Germany flying from bases in the UK, rather than France. The Halifax I and the Halifax II also had different fuel capacities, and the squadron flew both types.

We were briefed to go to Nuremberg, a total journey of more than 1,000 miles, and at the briefing, our new CO, Wing Commander Basil Robinson (Robinson had arrived from 78 Squadron to replace Collings in July), made a big point of saying that he did not want any of us landing away from base, which was becoming a habit. He didn't want his aircraft spread out all over the country which we understood. I had been given a special 'computer' – a sort of circular slide-rule – by Rolls-Royce and by my reckoning, however, given the air miles and the fuel load, there was no margin for error whatsoever, and so mentioned it to the wingco before we took off. He tartly replied that 'Group must know what they're doing'. Unfortunately, as events would unfold, they didn't!

Nuremberg, the second largest town in Bavaria, was the spiritual home of Nazi power, and an obvious high-priority 'morale' target. The destruction of morale was considered one of the four legitimate reasons for prosecuting the bombing campaign, behind attacks on transport, industry, and naval and military centres – all graded according to importance. In fairness, Nuremberg was as much a centre for manufacturing tanks, submarine engines, and electrical equipment, as well as anti-semitism.

The attack, the first to be mounted against the city, involved some 152 aircraft including nine Halifaxes and seven Stirlings. Contemporary reports suggest that the raid was far from a success, with some bombs dropping in villages more than 65 miles from the city, and a handful in a town nearly 100 miles away! Eight aircraft were lost, and five more crashed in England. One of these was our own Halifax L9579, the 49th of only 84 Mark I's ever built. It had a maximum fuel load of 1,552 gallons.

There was four minutes difference between the time our navigator said we would arrive over base, and the time I said we would run out of fuel. In the event, I was the one who was proved to be right! It wasn't entirely his fault. I kept the throttle settings and speed constant for maximum fuel efficiency on the way out and on the way back. You have to remember we had four engines, two on each side feeding off the fuel in their respective wing. But they don't consume fuel at exactly the same rate. What happened was that two of the engines on one wing packed up at the same time. This in itself wasn't a problem, but it meant that I had to go to the rear of the aircraft behind the rear spar to find the cross feed cock to transfer the fuel from the only tank that was still running fuel to all four engines, but by my calculations we were now running on fumes.

Although we got within sight of the airfield coming home, it was clear that we weren't going to make it. I told the skipper and he gave the order to bale out. That was all very well but on this particular flight, we had the added complication of carrying a second pilot, a skipper from 58 Squadron. We used to carry the Whitley skippers as co-pilots before they did the conversion course (from two engines to four). Being used to his own aircraft, this fellow had put on a full Irving suit – the big Irving top, the big Irving trousers – and he was a big lad himself. When Williams gave us the order to go this fellow sat in the hatch with his legs dangling over the edge. He then tried to dive through head-first, the end result being that he got stuck with his bottom thrusting up into the air. Len Thorpe, our wireless operator, was due to go next, and so climbed back up the steps to where the co-pilot's position was, and jumped straight down onto this fellow's backside and the pair of them went out like a cork out of a bottle!

By now the Halifax had sunk to around 1,000ft. The co-pilot, navigator and wireless op had left, leaving me and the skipper alone. Or so we thought. We still had just about enough time to get out so I went to get the skipper's parachute pack that was stowed in the lower compartment, under the step. (Since the Battle of Britain, Bomber Command had not had pilot type parachutes; our pilots wore an observer type harness with a separate pack.) When I got there, however, the 'chute was missing. I don't think it can have been secured very well, and probably got sucked out when the escape hatch was opened. I climbed back up and told him by which time we were so low that he had only one choice left, and that was to attempt a crash landing.

I opened the escape hatch above the pilot's head and then went amidships and opened the hatch there. To do so you had to lower a metal ladder, that was a rather solid structure (it was replaced in later models by a wire ladder). I was still clinging to this ladder when the aircraft finally went in. It hit me square on, but fortunately my face seemed to get squashed between the rungs so I wasn't badly hurt.

Williams displayed enormous skill in bringing the aircraft to earth without power, managing to 'glide' the aircraft close to the ground whilst keeping the nose up, ensuring the optimum lift with the minimal speed. The flaps had been selected down, but the undercarriage started to come down when the last engine stopped. The wind-milling props must have produced some hydraulic pressure. Williams killed the speed by dropping the flaps early, bringing the Halifax as close to the ground as he could, and as slow as he could, until he virtually 'sensed' rather than saw where the ground was and put the aircraft down.

I remember clearly the horrible rending of metal as the aircraft came to a halt. The skin of the Halifax makes a terrible noise when it is being torn apart, and it is not a comforting sound. Williams was well strapped in and braced, so he was able to undo his harness quickly and clamber out of the pilot's hatch. I was just at the point of getting out when our rear gunner suddenly appeared and said 'wait for me'. I didn't even know he was still with us! The three of us clambered out onto the wing and were going to get down but there were all these cattle charging around in front of us. In the whole episode, this was probably the only thing that actually frightened me, as I suppose it was so unexpected.

News of the crash landing reached the squadron that promptly dispatched two emergency vehicles to the scene: one apparently for the bodies, and one for the wounded. When they got there and found out that we were all unhurt, they left us to make our own way back in the van that brought out the guard.

Beyond a red-faced squadron commander, there was little fall-out from the Nuremberg debacle. Williams, with me trying my best to use every drop of fuel, had managed to keep the Halifax aloft for eight hours and 25 minutes. One more minute and we may have made it. As it happened, we were the only aircraft even to get close, Keith Cresswell and his crew only just managing to make the English coast.

After the excitement of the crash landing, Williams was given a new aircraft, L9580, the 70th Mark I built, in which we flew a series of air tests and then an uneventful sortie (on October 21) to the shipyards at Bremen. Five days later we successfully bombed Hamburg, Germany's second largest city and first port of the Reich, inflicting more damage and casualties than usual for raids during this period. The shipyards of Blohm & Voss and Deutsche Werft made a major contribution to the German war machine, and would feature frequently on the list of preferred targets.

I had never really known the meaning of 'fear', and as it happens it wasn't on operations that somebody first introduced me to that most unpleasant of sensations. Rather it was Leonard Cheshire, and his desire to go 'experimenting'.

A few months previously, Cheshire had nearly lost his own life and the lives of his crew with some pretty daft flying. He had been experimenting with the idea that German flak was more accurate because they could 'hear' our aircraft, and that helped with their ranging. He reasoned that if they couldn't hear you, you ran less risk of being hit. (This happened to coincide with photographs at the time that showed pictures of great acoustic listening devices that the RAF was apparently using to detect German bombers. Of course this was pure propaganda, to cover the development and success of radar. It might not have fooled the Germans, but it certainly seems to have fooled our Leonard!)

Anyway, one night he decided to try out his theory. Over the target he cut all four engines and went into a glide, trouble was, when he attempted to restart the engines he found that he couldn't. It was only by some miracle that he managed to get one going again and then another, and finally make it back to base but it was a foolhardy thing to do and he received a real rocket from the CO when he got back.

Unfortunately, Cheshire had clearly not fully learned his lesson, as my log book entry for October 29 attests, when he decided to scare the life out of me and a handful of my compatriots. Now Cheshire never struck me as a professional pilot, certainly not compared to people like Don Bennett with whom I flew later in the war. On the particular day in question, Cheshire strode into the crew room, I was still a corporal at the time, and asked whether any of us co-pilots or flight engineers had any experience of flying in an iced-up aircraft? Flying conditions were shocking; all flying had been cancelled, but for some reason I and a few others decided we'd go with him. What a mistake.

The take-off was simple enough, despite the dreadful conditions, and we began to climb steadily through the gloom. We were all on intercom, with me in the mid-ship position, when he started to play around with the heating, turning the hot air on and off on one of the engines until it seized. We dropped. He restarted it again and we climbed. He then proceeded to stop and re-start the engine several times until such time as I was thrown onto the ceiling and banged my head as he pushed the stick fully forward and put the aircraft into a dive. I was not impressed. I was pleased never to have to fly with him again. Paddy, his flight engineer, was welcome to him.

By the end of October I had completed 27 hours and 30 minutes of operations flying, and my log book was duly signed by Squadron Leader Cheshire for officer commanding B Flight. It was a happy month for the squadron in that there were no major incidents to report and no casualties. Though I didn't know it at the time, my tenure at 35 Squadron was rapidly coming to an end, although it would not be long before it was once again rekindled, and for a considerably longer period. In the meantime I flew only twice in November, non-operationally, and spent most of December with my fellow aircrew waiting to see whether the two German warships *Scharnhorst* and *Gneisenau* would make a dash for the open sea.

Unhappily the casualty rate increased considerably during that period with the loss of two crews in November – 20-year-old Pilot Officer Gordon Whittaker killed over Holland whilst on a Rover patrol and Flight Sergeant Jock Hamilton shot down and captured attacking Hamburg on the night of November 30/December 1. December was worse. Sergeant Gerald Grigg failed to return from Cologne on December 11/12, killed with all his crew whilst flying his 21st operation – one for every year of his life.

The CO, Wing Commander Basil Robinson, meanwhile nearly came to a sticky end on December 18 when his aircraft was hit by flak so badly over Brest that they were forced to ditch some 60 miles short of the English coast. They were later rescued. (Flying with him that day was 'Revs' Rivaz, famed gunner with Leonard Cheshire who wrote his own account of the war and this raid in the famous book *Tail Gunner.*)

On Boxing Day I went up with a young Canadian pilot, George Steinhauer, for some local flying and practice night landing, although there was more tragedy to come. The year ended with the loss of the popular flight commander, Squadron Leader Stuart 'Sam' Middleton DFC, last seen going down in a steep dive, again over Brest, having taken a direct hit to his port wing. An Auxiliary Air Force pilot, in peace-time Middleton had been a chartered accountant. He was the last casualty for the month, another victim of one of the 200 or more guns that protected the harbour, if not the guns of the ships he had been sent to attack. But by then, I had again been posted, and was on my way to join 102 Squadron, RAF Dalton.

CHAPTER THREE

CONVERTING

Straightaway there was a difference at 102 Squadron. At 35 Squadron I had been one of many, not remarkable in any way. Just one of the lads. Now suddenly I'm the engineer, the one with the knowledge and the experience, with my own office, talking on level terms with the pilots. Despite my relatively young age, my experience of four-engined bombers, and the Halifax especially, was enough to give me 'special' status. I was, for the first time in my life, a big fish in a small pond.

102 'Ceylon' Squadron had been formed in 1935 from B Flight of 7 Squadron, and had originally been equipped with the Heyford bomber before the first Whitleys began arriving in 1938. At the outbreak of war 102 Squadron began leaflet-dropping raids over Germany, losing its first crew on one such operation within the first week of hostilities being declared. Like the rest of Bomber Command, the squadron was not able to begin bombing raids until the Germans invaded Norway in April 1940. From then until the end of the war, 102 Squadron took part in the strategic bombing campaign, with only two breaks. The first came in September-October 1940, when the squadron was loaned to Coastal Command, and spent six weeks carrying out convoy escort duties from Prestwick. The second came at the start of 1942, by which time it had moved to Dalton, when the squadron began the process of converting from the Whitley to the Halifax.

Dalton had started life as meadowland hastily cleared to provide a satellite to neighbouring RAF Topcliffe, and was actually nearer to the village of Topcliffe than the station that bore its name! At first, Dalton was no more than a relief and dispersal landing ground until facilities were gradually improved and a concrete runway laid to enable 102 Squadron to make it its permanent home. Dalton was what they called a 'dispersed' camp, meaning that its buildings were 'dispersed' all over the countryside, and we were all issued with bicycles in order to get about. The aerodrome was just that: flight offices, crew rooms etc. and of course the aircraft dispersed all around the field. Living quarters were in various locations, being a few huts surrounding the ablutions and one main camp for the various messes.

In terms of aircraft, the Whitley had served the squadron proudly. But the Halifax offered them something new. It was to assist in this very process that 35 Squadron had been asked to provide two pilots, a flight engineer and a wireless op/air gunner to help 102 convert from the Whitley to the Halifax. We didn't have an aircraft, so ended up going by road. Our brief was simple: we were the chaps with the experience and we were expected to spread the gospel!

The conversion flight was officially formed on January 6, 1942, the first Halifax (a Mark II registered as R9390) having already been delivered the month before. In charge of the flight was an auxiliary reserve officer, Squadron Leader P. B. Robinson; his chief flying instructor was another Halton apprentice, Pilot Officer Wallace Lashbrook. Wally was quite a bit older than the rest of us. Although he was ex Halton, like me, he was second Entry I believe so to the rest of us he was positively ancient by comparison. He had also been with 35 Squadron, again like me, before coming to 102 so our paths had already crossed.

Wally Lashbrook was a veteran in almost every sense of the word. Born in 1913, he had entered the RAF in January 1929, graduating from Halton as LAC fitter (aircraft engines) two years later, being awarded the first fitters prize. His first posting was to RAF Station Mountbatten where he was also a contemporary and colleague of Lawrence of Arabia, with whom he shared a love of motorbikes. In 1933 Wally volunteered for overseas duty and was assigned to 100 TE Squadron. He moved with the squadron and from 1934-1936 was based in Selatar, Singapore as a fitter. In November 1936 he was selected for pilot training, initially with Scottish Aviation, Prestwick, flying Tiger Moths. From here in January of 1937 he graduated to 2 Flying Training School at Digby for advanced training on the Hawker Hart and Hawker Audax. The unit did not see heavy action and suffered few casualties before being posted to the Middle East in November of 1940.

With the conversion to the more modern aircraft Wally had already been posted to No 2 Ferry pool at Filton. By this time he had accumulated 369 flying hours. He stayed in this pool until mid-1940 ferrying 36 different types of aircraft and 375 in total including replacement Hurricane fighter aircraft to France just before the collapse. On September 1, 1940, at the height of the Battle of Britain, Wally was posted to 51 Squadron (4 Group) flying Whitley V's out of Dishforth, Yorkshire. By January 1941 he had completed 25 operations, and received the DFM. Posted to Malta, he took part in one of the first parachute drops of the war, transporting troops to attack the Calitri aqueduct in Italy. Returning to the UK he was posted to 35 Squadron where he had a series of adventures that earned him the respect of his fellow pilots and a commission to pilot officer. A serious motorcycle crash put him out of action for five months in the autumn of 1941, by which time his posting had come through initially to 28 Conversion Unit and then to 102 Squadron.

Wally began giving instruction to pilots almost immediately (records actually show that Lashbrook had begun conversion training for 102 Squadron crews in December before the conversion flight was officially in place) and he would invite me along either as engineer or second pilot.

The challenge of converting from two to four engines should not have been that great. It was probably much more of a challenge for the boys before the war converting from single-engined Hawker Hinds onto the then modern twin-engined Whitleys. That really took some guts. In terms of flying, it was just a question of getting used to a slightly bigger aircraft, and understanding its handling characteristics as well as its 'systems' (e.g. its hydraulics). It was also a case of knowing where everything was. Before flying any new aircraft you had to undertake what they call a 'blindfold test' and that means being able to locate all of the essential switches and dials (e.g. the magneto switches, the throttles, the engine feather buttons, fire extinguishers, fuel cocks etc.) that you might need in an emergency. You would also read the pilot's notes, of course, that would recommend take-off and landing speeds, approach speeds, angles and such like.

Early on in the conversion training, I would lecture pilots and engineers under instruction on the Halifax fuel, pneumatic, hydraulic and electrical systems; later when the pilot was taking his first solo, I might sit in the co-pilot's seat. The Whitley captains would typically come to us for conversion after they had completed around 20 trips, so they were all quite experienced flyers, but even so it could be hairy at times. On one occasion, after I had been on the squadron some time, a pilot on his first daylight solo managed to break the undercarriage. That same evening, with a first night solo, the pilot managed to swing off the runway and break the aircraft but luckily not himself. Fortunately two near-disasters in one day was the exception not the rule.

My log book details a series of test flights and circuits and landings, checking out both fledgling aircraft and pupils. Not surprisingly, and quite correctly, priority in training was primarily given to the squadron commander, flight commanders and senior crews. On the morning of January 29, I flew as engineer to the A Flight commander, Squadron Leader Griffiths, undertaking two circuits and landings and a weather test; later that afternoon, whilst flying with a Sergeant Boothright in a new Halifax II (R9488), training had to be cut short when the undercarriage failed to retract – a not untypical problem that gave me little cause for alarm (it was the sort of thing I was used to) but no doubt spooked the pilot. February followed a similar pattern, Squadron Leader Griffiths being a regular captain and a new name, Sergeant Malkin, appearing on the flying orders for the first – but by no means the last – time.

In February 1942 there had also been a seismic change at Bomber Command headquarters. Sir Richard Peirse, the commander-in-chief, had been removed from office after being held directly accountable for a disastrous raid three months earlier when 37 aircraft had been lost cheaply – and perhaps even unnecessarily – due to poor weather. Temporary command passed to Air Vice-Marshal Baldwin in a caretaker role before the permanent appointment of a new C-in-C, 'Butch' Harris. It would be several months, however, before the full significance of Harris' promotion would impact on my operational career, and chances of survival.

I was once again floored by a bout of influenza towards the end of March. What started as a headache and mild sore throat soon developed into a temperature of 101 and nine days in the sick bay. Having been discharged at the end of the month, I was then immediately sent on seven days leave to convalesce before returning to duties in April, by which time the squadron had sufficient numbers of new pilots and crews trained that it was deemed ready for operations. It was also, however, the month when the unit suffered its first fatalities, with two of the recently converted pilots – 26-year-old Flight Lieutenant Harry Williams and Sergeant John Morris, an Australian – killed when their Halifax (R9488) stalled and crashed into the ground near Ripon. At around lunchtime on that same day, April 14, I was detailed for an air test with no less a man than the squadron commander himself, Wing Commander Bintley.

Wing Commander Sydney Bruce Bintley AFC (and later DSO), one of the Reserve of Air Force Officers (RAFO), had been granted his short service commission on August 9, 1937 and was in air operations from the outset, being mentioned in a dispatch by his superiors as early as February 1940 whilst still a flying officer. Now a 29-year-old wing commander, he had taken over command of 102 Squadron officially on January 1, 1942 and was already proving an effective CO. I came across a good many of his rank and background who tended to have a chip on their shoulder but not Bintley. He was popular and well-liked.

For the night's operations the target was northern France, and specifically the harbour installations around Le Havre. The six-hour flight went off without a hitch, the Halifax (9494) landing safely back at base at 03.05 hours. Whilst there was no damage to any of the squadron's aircraft, there was perhaps even less damage to the enemy, with all of the bombs from the 23 bombers taking part in the raid falling in open countryside.

The next day I was assigned to Squadron Leader Griffiths for what was termed a 'minor operation' in Bomber Command parlance to attack the U-boat pens and harbour of Lorient. Again there was little damage reported, either to the squadron or the enemy. A similar minor operation, this time involving 39 aircraft, was arranged for the night of April 24, and this time I was paired with a 21-year-old Flight Sergeant Stanley Morgan.

The squadron lost two further pilots before the month was out: Sergeant John Barber, shot down by flak over Dunkirk, and Flight Sergeant Larry Carr who fell victim to Oberleutnant Reinhold Eckardt of 7/NJG7 on the way to Cologne. Carr survived, Barber did not.

That same evening another skipper and his crew were shot down from 10 Squadron. All baled out successfully. Fate would determine that three would be captured, and four would escape back to Britain. One of the four was the commanding officer of 10 Squadron, and future leader of 8 Group, Pathfinder force, Donald Bennett.

I had been great friends with Bennett's flight engineer, Flight Sergeant Colgan, while he had been at 35 Squadron. We were as different as chalk and cheese, really. I was the youngest on the squadron and he was one of the oldest. We were also from totally different backgrounds. He was a Yorkshireman from a coalmining family, and I remember him taking me once to see his family. We went out to the local mineworkers' social club and you can imagine I stuck out like a sore thumb. Colgan had started in the RAF at the lowest possible place you could, as a fitter's mate (categorised as a group five). It had taken him years to get to become a flight mechanic (a group two) before finally becoming a fitter proper (a group one). After that he volunteered to become a flight engineer. He was the man who Bennett – not one to bestow many favours – credits with saving his life when they were shot down attacking the *Tirpitz*.

Bennett, with Colgan at his side, had taken off from RAF Lossiemouth and led the squadron low over the North Sea to

Norway. On reaching the target, and on the bombing run, the crew encountered the German smoke screen at 400 feet, which all but obscured the battleship below. Although Bennett caught a glimpse of the ship's superstructure for a fraction of a second, it was not long enough to let the mines go, and so he headed out of the fjord in order to turn around and make a second run.

The aircraft (an English electric-built Halifax IIA-B, W1041) was all the time being fired upon from both sides of the fjord as well as by *Tirpitz* itself. As the aircraft climbed out of Fættenfjord it was set upon by all the flak batteries situated on the hills around the fjords. The aircraft received a hit and a fire broke out on the wing behind the starboard inner engine. The rear gun turret had also sustained damage resulting in the gunner, F/L How, receiving cuts to his face.

Bennett started to gain some altitude and ordered the crew to prepare to bale out. The mines were jettisoned and Bennett turned the aircraft east in the direction of Sweden. At this point the fire on the wing appeared to die down, and it looked for a moment as if they might be saved. It was but a short reprise, however, as the fire once again took hold, this time with increased ferocity. The starboard inner engine then cut out, and the starboard wheel fell down into the landing position making the aircraft very unstable. It was at this point that Bennett gave the order to go. The navigator, Sergeant Eyles, was first to leave the aircraft, followed by the second pilot Sergeant Walmsley. The two wireless operators, Sergeants Forbes and Murray went next.

In Bennett's book, *Pathfinder*, he describes the uncomfortable fact dawning upon him that he wasn't wearing his parachute, and how surprised and relieved he was when Colgan suddenly appeared and clipped his 'chute to his chest, giving him a chance to escape. He says that Colgan risked his own life in doing this, before heading off back down the fuselage to help the wounded rear gunner out of his turret and out of the aircraft, before baling out himself. (Colgan was captured and spent the rest of the war as a POW in Stalag Luft III.) Had he not acted as he did, we might never have had a Pathfinder force – certainly not in the mould in which it ultimately materialised.

The next night (April 28/29), I was back in the saddle with Griffiths to attack the naval town of Kiel, the principal base of the German fleet, and at the time viewed by some as a 'nursery target' where freshly trained crews could gain their first operational experience. We had the distinction of being the only Halifax to take part in that raid, although not the only Halifax flying. Two, both from 35 Squadron, were lost on a separate raid that same evening against the *Tirpitz*.

May kicked off with a cross-country with the recently promoted Hank Malkin, who had moved one further step up the ladder from sergeant to flight sergeant. Although I didn't know it at the time, Hank and I would share many near misses in the months ahead as we steadily became part of a regular crew, but for the time being the pace of training – and operations – began to build.

As each new Halifax arrived, one of the faithful Whitleys departed. The officer in command of the conversion training, Squadron Leader Robinson, had a scare on May 11 when he was forced to crash land Halifax V9982 at Pick Hill, Northallerton, causing injury to himself and two trainee pilots. Another Halifax (W1099) crashed on May 20 when an engine overheated (although the crew were uninjured), and a further aircraft (W7677) only just made it home having been attacked by a Messerschmitt 110 nightfighter over the Dutch coast. Its pilot, 'Batch' Batchelder received the Distinguished Flying Medal for his night's work. As it happened I missed all of this excitement as my run of bad luck with illness continued. Conjunctivitis, which had plagued me since my early days at Halton, returned to both eyes, and I had to bathe them in hot water every three hours. The MO also painted the conjunctive with silver nitrate until after nine days of treatment I was sufficiently recovered to be sent away (once again) on seven days convalescence.

New flight engineers began appearing on a regular basis; one I remember well because he only had one leg. The story goes that he was a pre-war regular who had lost his leg in a motorcycle accident early in the war. It was unusual, of course, for the air force to let you stay with such a disability, but they did, and put him in charge of the station workshop on the basis that it wouldn't involve having to clamber over any aircraft. What they didn't bargain for, however, was that he would soon tire of being in the workshop and apply to become a flight engineer. I am not quite sure how he passed the selection criteria. I think at that stage in the war, if you were mad enough to volunteer, they would take you.

At a squadron level, we were not entrusted with – or even particularly bothered by – any master strategy devised by our commander-in-chief. We certainly didn't know that there was soon to be a dramatic and one might even suggest melodramatic shift in Bomber Command's effort: the era of the 1,000 bomber raids was about to begin.

Harris felt he needed to make a bold statement about the role and importance of his new command. The propaganda impact of putting more than 1,000 bombers in the air over Germany on a single night was an ambition that he proposed could be realised if he added those crews close to finishing their operational or conversion training to the 400 or so crews he already had on his front-line strength. In the event, making the numbers wasn't the issue; getting them over the target within a given period and within a given degree of accuracy was the problem. This problem was solved by the innovation that was the 'bomber stream' and a tactic that would eventually form the basis for standard Bomber Command operations for most of the rest of the war.

Another issue was the target. Hamburg was the favourite, home to the Fatherland's U-boat building machinery. Weather conditions, however, necessitated a change in target. Hamburg could wait, and in its place came Cologne, another great inland port with miles of docks and acres of marshalling yards – one of the chief transport targets in Germany. So the scene was set. History was about to be made. And I missed it!

Whilst I was in the air in the small hours of the night and early morning of May 30, bombing the Gnome & Rhône factory in Paris from less than 4,000ft with yet another new pilot, Flight Lieutenant Welsh, the teleprinters were chattering their orders to the four principal bomber groups and two training groups that operation Millennium was about to begin.

The raid was set for a take-off later that evening. Perhaps that was why I wasn't on the battle order.

Luckily for me, although not the Germans, the raid on Cologne was the first of what was to become a series of 1,000 bomber raids over the next few months, and the second was scheduled for June 1/2. This time I was down to be part of the force to attack Essen, and again flying with Flight Lieutenant Welsh. We took off without any problems but only a little way into the flight, the pilot kept complaining that he had ear trouble. Indeed it became so serious that it was soon evident that we would have to turn back. He obviously hadn't cleared his ears properly, probably when we went so low over the target two days before. Anyway, the upshot was that we missed the raid, and yet another historic event went by without me playing any part!

To be properly accurate, not all 1,000 aircraft were in fact available for that night's operations, and the damage done was relatively minor. Casualties amongst the attacking force were relatively high, with 31 bombers missing and many others damaged beyond repair. One such aircraft came from 102 Squadron: Halifax R9529 crashed near Düsseldorf, killing all onboard including the skipper, 20-year-old Sergeant Edmund Newell. The following night a second Halifax R9532 was severely damaged by flak, crash landing at Dalton and breaking its back in the process. The Australian pilot and his crew escaped unhurt. That same evening Warrant Officer Frank Holmes, a 25-year-old Canadian, ditched his Halifax (R9491) in the sea near Harwich. I went up as engineer to Flight Sergeant Duff to look for them, scanning the vast expanse of ocean for more than four hours in the hope of seeing a dinghy or any sign of wreckage but without any luck. Holmes and five of his crew are still officially posted as 'missing'.

June was proving to be a busy month. On June 5, I found myself crewed with Hank Malkin, a pairing that was shortly to become a regular fixture. I liked Hank. He was a Canadian from Vancouver, a good looking so and so and he knew it. He used to spend most of his time off duty chasing girls. What I would say about Hank, however, was that he was a good pilot and a good flyer. He had a real panache about him and that gave me confidence when we were flying. Early operations with Hank to Essen (June 5) and Osnabrück (June 19) proved uneventful. It would not always be the case.

In the meantime, there were further distractions. In the middle of June the whole squadron upped-sticks for the short 10-minute flight to our new home Topcliffe, from whence the squadron had come only seven months before. I had mixed feelings about the move: I was happy because Topcliffe was a permanent site with real hangars and decent accommodation. What I wasn't happy about was that I had to leave my little Triumph car behind. I couldn't take it with me.

Actually to say that I couldn't take it with me is perhaps a little unfair, or at least requires a further note of explanation. It wasn't that I wasn't allowed to have my own car on the base, but rather that an incident was rather obliging me to leave it behind. It was a wonderful little car that had a free-wheel system – a knob on the panel that you turned and then lifted your foot off the accelerator such that it ran by itself, rather like a modern-day cruise control. Anyway, let's just say that one day I had a little trouble with the free-wheel system and ended up running the car into a ditch on one of the tiny lanes than ran from the mess to the airfield. I left it there when we were posted. It was a pity, because I had paid £70 for that car, which was quite a bit of money in those days.

On June 26 I thought I would at last get to take part in a 1,000 bomber raid but my efforts were again thwarted when, flying with Wing Commander Bintley, we were obliged to return home early on three engines, failing to reach our target, Bremen. The next night, however, I managed to get to the German dockyards in the company of Flight Lieutenant Hamilton and return without incident. A third attack on Bremen, again with Bintley, was also successfully concluded, albeit that one petrol tank was holed, meaning that I kept an even closer look on the dials than usual, ensuring as little of the fuel was wasted as possible.

This was a painful period for the squadron, losing no fewer than seven crews in the space of 10 days: Flight Sergeant Charles Barr, a Canadian from Quebec with whom I had flown a two-hour cross-country only a few weeks before, was shot down and killed over Essen on June 17. He died alongside fellow Canadian Warrant Officer William Davies and crew. Sergeant 'Batch' Batchelder was also missing, but later reported as a prisoner of war.

Flight Sergeant (later Pilot Officer) Stanley Morgan, with whom I had flown a single operation in April, was killed over Bremen, the same night (June 25/26) that the 20-year-old Canadian Frederick Duff was killed. Indeed this was a dreadful night for 102 Squadron, losing no fewer than four aircraft. Out of 23 aircrew posted as 'missing', only three survived to become prisoners of war, one of whom was later killed by friendly fire when POWs on the march were mistaken for a column of enemy troops. Within Stan Morgan's crew, the dead included Pilot Officer Patrick Robinson, whose father had won the Victoria Cross as a Royal Navy lieutenant commander for single-handedly attacking a gun emplacement during the ill-fated Dardanelles campaign in 1915.

My time at Topcliffe was only short. Within two months the squadron had again moved to Pocklington from where they would see out the war. Meanwhile in July a short period of leave was followed by a programme of flying comprising a classic mixture of testing aircraft and aircrew, instructing flight engineers 'under training' and conducting further sea searches for aeroplanes that would never be found, and whose crews would ultimately be noted as lost without trace. I flew only one operation in July, a relatively long-haul to Düsseldorf in the second pilot's seat with Flight Sergeant Boothright in command. I remember little of the adventure, other than that we were diverted on our return to Swinderby.

New descriptions began appearing in my log book throughout a busy August illustrating the diversity of my role whilst officially now part of 102 Squadron's Conversion Flight: circuits and bumps (C&B), local flying, air firing, dual tests, and overshoot tests on three engines. One entry for August 17 with Pilot Officer Drummond and Flight Sergeant Towse simply states: 'C&B, Dual & Solo. Aircraft written off!' A last hurrah to Osnabrück with my flight commander, Squadron Leader Robinson, brought up my 15th operation, a total of more than 100 hours of operational flying.

It was time for a new challenge, a new group, and a return to old friends.

CHAPTER FOUR

PATHFINDING

The 35 Squadron to which I returned on September 1, 1942, was a very different squadron from the one I had left eight months before. Eight months in the duration of a war was a lifetime – quite literally as it turned out to some of my former colleagues.

My casual enquiries into old friends more often than not brought sad news. Flight Sergeant George Steinhauer, the jovial 22-year-old from Saskatchewan, had been killed on March 30/31, 1942 attacking the *Tirpitz*. George had apparently had something of a premonition that he would die, verging on an obsession with the ship that was known in various circles as 'the beast'. There was even a suggestion that George had deliberately set out that night with the intention of never coming back, although the idea appears fanciful in the extreme. What is known for certain is that he was killed along with two other 35 Squadron crews, and the official raid report states that the *Tirpitz* was left undamaged.

But there had been a much bigger and more significant change to 35 Squadron during my absence. No longer was it part of Air Vice-Marshal Roddy Carr's 4 Group. Now it was one of the new elite Pathfinder squadrons, under the command of a certain Donald Bennett.

I was never quite sure how we ended up 'volunteering' for Pathfinders. Hank Malkin was one of those pilots who always wanted to prove himself against the best and so the Pathfinders was the obvious next step. He had put it to his crew but his flight engineer had not wanted to go so he asked me if I would go with him instead. Having been at 35 Squadron before, I jumped at the chance of going back. And so we did. The rest of the crew comprised three English sergeants and a Canadian navigator with whom I was to become good friends, Flight Sergeant Carl Sorsdahl.

By 1942, bomber crews were in no doubt of the hazards that faced them in an operational tour, and their chances of survival. Flying over the darkened skies of Nazi occupied territories night after night, often for seven, eight or even nine hours at a stretch was enough to test the endurance of aircraft and aircrew alike. A full tour, for those few miracle men who had survived the first onslaught, was 30 operations, perhaps 300 flying hours. Outwardly that doesn't sound very much, but imagine if that for every second in every minute in every hour of those 300 hours you could die at any time, either as a result of enemy action or an aircraft malfunction, and you begin to see why your nerves might be worn a little thin by the end of it all.

Life on a bomber station could be cruel. You could be out with colleagues from the squadron one evening, watching a film, and then the next night the chap that you were sitting next to was missing believed killed. It was a sobering thought. I was affected when the son of a family friend was killed. We had been at school together and he was a good pal. He was shot down over Hamburg and his body never found. It was something you tried not to dwell upon, but it prayed upon your mind nonetheless.

For the first time, chances of survival began to be discussed. It was reckoned in the early days of 35 Squadron that your life expectancy was three weeks, something not dissimilar to the slaughterhouse of the Western Front in the First World War. Official figures were published, but the crews knew best. We could transfer official figures into empty beds, and missing faces in the mess for the post-op meal or at breakfast. For the period 1939-1942, the chances of any man surviving just one operational tour was one in three. The odds against surviving a second tour (a further 20 operations) grew slimmer with each subsequent sortie.

Despite this, examples of aircrew actually losing their nerve and refusing to fly at that time – and indeed throughout the entire war – were the exception not the rule. The 'condition', if

that is the right word, was known as lacking in moral fibre –
abbreviated to LMF – and defined as the state when an airman
had forfeited the confidence of his commanding officer. It
meant instant disgrace, and immediate removal of their aircrew
brevet, to many, the harshest punishment of all.

Of course some people did go LMF but I can honestly say
that I never knew of any personally. I did come across a man
at Eastchurch once who had had enough; he used to come into
the canteen where my mother worked in Sheerness. Some were
obviously just unlucky. They'd had a nasty experience and
couldn't cope. That fact was that you just didn't know how
you would react unless you were in that position yourself. I
never held it against any of them. You never knew their story.
When it did happen on a squadron, the individuals would just
disappear overnight, but in wartime people just disappeared
anyway, so you didn't really notice.

Sometimes airmen could be persuaded from not going LMF,
especially if you had a good adjutant, and in many ways I think
they had the toughest job of all. They tended to be a little older
than the rest of us, sometimes as old as 30, and better able to
deal with whatever life threw their way. A good adjutant you
could talk to about anything, and he might be able to deal with
a situation without causing a great hue and cry.

The efforts of the bomber boys were remarkable; their
results, however, were entirely disproportionate to the
sacrifices being made. This was highlighted in the now
infamous Butt Report conducted by a Mr D. M. B. Butt of the
War Cabinet Secretariat. Butt had been commissioned by Lord
Cherwell, previously Professor Sir Frederick Lindemann and
scientific advisor to the prime minister, to attempt a statistical
analysis of the results of our efforts to bomb Germany. His
findings were alarming, to say the very least.

Butt examined 650 photographs from night operations
conducted between June 2 and July 25 1941, relating to 100
separate raids on 28 different targets. He concluded the
following: that of those aircraft recorded as attacking the
target, only one in three got within five miles; over the French
ports, the proportion was two in three, but over Germany as a
whole, the proportion was one in four. Over the Ruhr, this

figure fell to one in 10. Conditions played an important part in the success or otherwise of each raid: in a full moon, the proportion that got to within five miles of the target was two in five; in the new moon it was one in 15. In the absence of haze, the proportion was over one half, whereas over thick haze it was only one in 15. Flak and fighter defences also impacted on performance: an increase in the intensity of AA fire was said to reduce the number of aircraft getting within five miles of their target in the ratio of three to two. Most alarming of all: all of these figures relate only to those aircraft recorded as attacking the target, not those who failed to reach, find or bomb the enemy. The proportion of the total sorties which reached within five miles, therefore, was less than a third.

The good Mr Butt was most thorough in his analysis and insistent that his results should be qualified with two further statements: that this figure of one third related only to those who believed they had bombed the primary target. Some 6,103 aircraft were despatched in the raids that were evaluated, of these only 4,065 completed an 'attack' – i.e. a return of 66%. Thus of the total number of aircraft despatched, it was not one third that reached the target area but rather one fifth. He also observed that in defining the target area for the purpose of his enquiry as having a radius of five miles, an area of over 75 square miles was taken. His findings state: 'The proportion of aircraft actually dropping their bombs on built-up areas must be very much less, but what this proportion is, however, cannot be indicated by the study of night photographs.'

Lord Cherwell, in presenting these findings to Churchill, conceded that the figures might not be wholly accurate, but suggested – rather presciently as it happens – that they were sufficiently striking to emphasise the supreme importance of improving navigation.

The whole issue of accuracy had been discussed at length and the idea of a vanguard of bombers with either the proven experience or skill to lead others to the target was a popular topic of conversation in squadron mess room and Air Ministry committee room alike. The germ of an idea for a separate force became a seed that grew, cultivated by a 34-year-old temporary group captain named Sydney Bufton. Bufton had been a squadron commander early in the war, and was under no illusions as to the effectiveness of his crews' efforts. Appointed to the Air Ministry in 1942 as deputy director of bombing operations, he vigorously set about canvassing support from the great and the good for the creation of a separate 'target marking' force made up of hand-picked crews from the main force squadrons. His ideas eventually found favour with the Chief of Air Staff, Lord Portal, who directed the C-in-C Bomber Command, 'Butch' Harris, to put Bufton's ideas into practice.

History tells us that Harris resisted. He argued that if the best crews were taken from the main force squadrons, it would strip them of their best men and future leaders, thereby making them less effective. Morale would also suffer as a result, whereas leaving the men in place and having target marker experts within each squadron would create healthy rivalry. There was an argument also that elite squadrons at the vanguard of a bombing operation would be singled out for special attention by the German defenders, and take a much higher percentage of casualties. Even though Harris had the support in his views from all of his Group commanders, he did not win the argument, and in the end was ordered to do as he was told. He did win one argument, however. The name championed for this new enterprise was the Target Marking force; Harris rejected this in favour of the Pathfinder force. He even decreed that the airmen should have their own badge, a winged eagle, to be worn on their breast pocket.

In finding an appropriate commander, Bufton recommended one of the war's greatest commanders, Basil Embry. Despite his credentials, and for reasons now lost in the past, Embry was not selected, his place instead going to the mercurial Australian, Donald Bennett. Harris had known Bennett since 1931, and although very young to become a group commander (Bennett was 31 whereas the average age of his contemporaries was 56), his technical knowledge and personal operational ability was considered as 'altogether exceptional'.

The Pathfinders officially began life on July 5, 1942 as a unit reporting directly to C-in-C Bomber Command. For aircraft and crews it poached four squadrons from within the existing group structure: No 7 from 3 Group (John Baldwin), No 83 from 5 Group (Alec Coryton), No 156 from 1 Group (Edward Rice), and No 35 from 4 Group. It also had a further squadron, No 109, designated for 'special purposes' that was not yet affiliated to any particular group.

There were notable differences between Pathfinders and main force crews. A 'normal' Bomber Command crew signed up for a tour of 30 operations, after which they were 'rested', often at an operational training unit (OTU). A second tour of 20 operations would then follow, after which the man could not be made to return to operations if he didn't wish. Pathfinders, however, were different. We could not be rested after 'only' 30 trips but rather they set a minimum 'tariff' for Pathfinder crews, after some further debate, at 45 operations. Given that I had already flown 15, that meant in effect it was like starting my tour again. There were some perks, however. Aircrew were elevated in rank, and therefore pay. Further promotions were virtually guaranteed.

The new Pathfinder force (PFF) was to be headquartered in Huntingdon, and its squadrons were dispersed around the airfields of Cambridgeshire, Huntingdonshire, Bedfordshire and the immediate surrounds. I was posted to RAF Graveley, a former 3 Group site that had become operational in the spring of 1942. It had been transferred to 35 Squadron in August, and the squadron flew its first operational sortie – and indeed suffered the Pathfinders' first official casualties – on the night of August 18/19. I arrived two weeks later, joining A Flight, commanded by Squadron Leader Jack Kerry DFC.

There was little time to settle in, and we were on operations the first night we arrived. We did some local flying in the early afternoon and then took off to attack Karlsruhe at 22:35. It was an uneventful trip personally, although we had to land at Wyton, one of our neighbouring bases, on our return. As a Pathfinder operation, it was extremely successful and caused extensive damage to the target.

Two more operations followed in rapid succession, to Bremen and Duisberg, the former being significant in that it was the first time the Pathfinders began to split their force into defined roles: 'illuminators' to light up the area with white flares; 'visual markers' to drop coloured flares once they had positively identified the aiming point; and 'backers-up' who dropped incendiary bomb loads as early as possible on the coloured flares so as to encourage those in the main stream to do the same. This would form the basis of many of the pathfinding operations in the immediate future.

Then came the night we were briefed to attack Frankfurt.

I recall that there was some confusion as regards our target but in the event we went to attack the Opel tank factory and a factory that made tyres (Michelin). We were one of nearly 250 aircraft flying that night with a track that took us over Luxembourg. It was there that the trouble started. My log book entry for that evening is matter of fact: 'Ops PFF. Frankfurt. Shot up by e/a (enemy aircraft) over Luxembourg. Lost one engine. Captain wounded. Returned to base.' At the time it was considerably more frightening than it sounds.

The Pathfinders were unable to locate Frankfurt accurately, and as a result, most of the bombing fell in the town of Rüsselsheim more than 15 miles away. Indeed only a handful of bombs fell on the city itself, and most of those were probably more by luck than design. But at the time I had other things to worry about.

We were 10 miles north of Aachen over Luxembourg when Sergeant Stanton, our rear gunner, reported an enemy fighter. It was playing silly beggars, switching on and off its green formation lights and white rear lights. It was about 1,000 yards away and then closed to 800 yards, still switching his lights off and on. Then they went out and he opened fire. The aircraft was hit in the fuselage between the second pilot and the navigator's position. The port inner engine propeller was also damaged, and being made of wood, it splintered and shed most of one blade.

A rotating propeller acts like a flywheel: with one blade severely damaged, the propeller is out of balance creating a tremendous vibration that if left unchecked can very soon cause severe structural damage. My problem was to determine which engine was damaged and stop it. The instruments were unreadable, and we were still under attack from the fighter trying to finish us off. The only thing I could do was brace myself between the fuselage wall and the step up to the captain's seat. As the fight continued, Hank was taking evasive action by corkscrewing all over the sky ('corkscrewing' was a standard flying manoeuvre to evade a stalking fighter). Meanwhile, I used the prop pitch control levers to find which one changed the vibration frequency, then feathered the rogue engine and turned off its fuel supply. I cannot describe my relief; the thought of an engine running at 2,650rpm coming loose with the prop still turning just a few feet away and likely to fracture fuel and other fluid lines was more than a little worrying and would most likely be fatal.

More importantly, though, our skipper was hit when one of the cannon shells came through the cockpit, passed under my left arm and hit Malkin in the leg. It wasn't a life-threatening wound but we were worried nonetheless.

Hank continued to throw the aircraft around and as he did the nightfighter – a twin-engined Messerschmitt 110 – flew over our mid-upper gunner who let loose with two and three second bursts which appeared to make contact, as he saw the German dive vertically down to port. (The fighter was later confirmed as destroyed.) Our Halifax was most unstable at this point, both as a result of the damage we had sustained to the propellers and our skipper. With his wounded leg, Hank had real trouble with the rudders, applying the necessary pressure, and keeping the aircraft from skidding. The Halifax struggled at the best of times with stability because of the configuration of its rudders and fins. Landing was obviously going to be a problem.

I worked with Hank to help him all I could. He effectively did all of the steering and I sorted out the throttles, flaps and control settings so that we could bring her down in one piece. The Halifax appeared to be very unstable, and another of the engines was vibrating wildly. I tried reducing the power to see if that made any difference, but it was clear there was a serious problem. I began to question whether we could get down before the whole thing came apart. Luckily we did, thanks to a masterly piece of flying from Hank.

Hank's efforts that night were sufficient to impress our squadron commander, Jimmy Marks, and his immediate superiors, the citation for Hank's Distinguished Flying Cross summarising the operation most succinctly:

> "One night in September, 1942, Pilot Officer Malkin, as captain of a Halifax aircraft, was detailed to attack a target at Frankfurt. When 80 miles away from the target area, his aircraft was attacked by an enemy nightfighter and much damage was sustained. Pilot Officer Malkin, although wounded in the leg by splinters from an explosive cannon shell, took evasive action and enabled his air gunners to return fire which caused the enemy aircraft to break away. Pilot Officer Malkin set course for home and, although suffering much pain, brought his aircraft back to base safely where he made a masterly landing."

We were indeed lucky to have made it home in one piece. An inspection of the Halifax after landing revealed that five out of the eight engine bearing bolts had sheared, and the engine might indeed have parted company with the wing at any moment.

Although Hank's wounds were not serious, they were sufficient to keep him off operations for nearly three weeks, during which time the squadron was to experience one of its worst tragedies – the loss of its commanding officer – Jimmy Marks – the first Pathfinder CO to be killed in action.

James Hardy Marks, Jimmy to his friends, was a deserved legend in the Bomber Command annals. A tall, fair-haired and well-built young man, Marks came from Sawbridgeworth on the Hertfordshire/Essex border. He had excelled at school in cricket and football, and an early passion to fly was fulfilled when he obtained his civilian flying ticket and was commissioned into the RAF on May 9, 1937. Upon the outbreak of war he was immediately in the thick of the action, flying deep penetration leaflet raids over Poland for which he was mentioned in a dispatch as early as January 1940. He won his first DFC[5] during the battle for France in May 1940, and a particular operation on May 20 in which he was detailed to attack an important road bridge. He carried out no fewer than three runs over the target to ensure the success of his mission.

Marks was one of the original 'press-on' types that so much has been written about. One night he was attacking a target, long before the Pathfinders were formed, and because of the weather and poor visibility, he was having trouble identifying the aiming point. He flew around the target area for more than an hour until conditions improved sufficiently for him to deliver an attack.

My friend Hamish Mahaddie in his memoirs (*Hamish: the story of a Pathfinder*) recounts a similar story that reveals Jimmy's early pathfinding credentials, a full two years before the formal Pathfinder squadrons were formed. Marks at the time was a flying officer with 77 Squadron, flying the twin-engined Whitleys. The squadron was briefed to attack troop concentrations in a wood near Rotterdam. Marks suggested that if they made a time-and-distance run from Rotterdam to the target, and then all dropped a flare, the bombers that followed would be assured of accurate bombing. Mahaddie writes:

"The interesting thing about this – in my experience the first ever co-ordinated attempt to find a target – was that despite the assurance of all the enthusiasts to the scheme that the run was made with great care, not one of a dozen or more taking part in this quite unofficial experiment claimed to have seen one of the other's flares or Very lights."

Marks, it should be noted, was undeterred by this initial failure, and tried again the following evening with more promising results. Appointed flight lieutenant on October 8, 1940, Marks survived a particularly difficult trip to Emden in April 1941 when his Whitley was cornered by a nightfighter over the target. The official report records:

---

[5]Marks' DFC was gazetted on July 9, 1940 in the same batch as two future Victoria Cross holders – Guy Gibson of Dambusters fame, and Leonard Trent who later took part in the Great Escape.

"He was just about to bomb when he was attacked from the rear by a nightfighter; the first burst hit the starboard engine, which stopped, thereby immobilising the rear turret (the turret relied on the engines for power). A second attack from below would have had far more serious consequences but for the protection offered by the 500lb bombs (!). On its final attack from head on, the nightfighter approached so close that it is presumed that it must have struck the rudder of the Whitley with its wing. Half of the rudder was severed completely, and when last seen, the fighter was banking over steeply in a dive as though one wing was damaged.

At this time, in spite of jettisoning bombs, the aircraft had lost height to 700 feet, and the Captain decided to make for Norfolk, and at this height, limped across some 50 miles of hostile and occupied territory. The air observer pulled up the floorboards and discovered one 500lb bomb, which had not dropped. This he released by hand, after which the aircraft climbed gradually to 1,000 feet and a successful landing was made at Bircham Newton."

Jimmy's efforts were recognised with his first Distinguished Service Order, gazetted on September 23, 1941, whilst an acting squadron leader of 58 Squadron. Promoted wing commander on March 12, 1942, he was posted from 10 OTU to take over command of 35 Squadron, succeeding Basil Robinson. At 23, he was at that time the youngest wing commander in the RAF.

He was, as expected, immediately leading from the front. On an operation against the *Tirpitz* in April 1942, he ignored the heavy flak barrage to press home an attack at less than 200 feet, releasing his bombs on or very close to the mighty warship. He had the honour of playing host to King George VI and Queen Elizabeth, as well as the Prime Minister Winston Churchill when they visited to hear first hand the magnificent work being carried out by the squadron. He was honoured too for his squadron to be chosen as one of the first of the Pathfinder squadrons, recalling with pride that of the 150 aircrew under his command at the time, all but seven were happy to follow his lead, even though many were already coming to the end of their operational tours and a period of relative safety.

On September 19, the target was Saarbrücken, a relatively modest raid involving 118 aircraft. Five were shot down, including two Halifax IIs, one (W7657) piloted by Jimmy Marks. As I understand it they were attacked by a nightfighter (an Me 110) from below (using Schräge Musik – an upward-firing canon) and he scored strikes on the port mainplane as well as setting fire to the number five and six fuel tanks. The ailerons were jammed and the fuselage was set on fire. Marks gave the order to bale out but only three managed to make it out before the aircraft crashed in flames. It was a great loss both to the squadron, and to the Pathfinders, and it was keenly felt at the time. It was doubly bad because we not only lost our CO, but we also lost the squadron's navigation leader (24-year-old Flight Lieutenant Alan Child DFC) and gunnery leader (Pilot Officer Richard Leith-Hay-Clark, 25).

Marks' loss on his 68th operation was a tremendous blow, and his selfless act in staying at the controls of his aircraft to allow others time to escape might have been recognised with a higher award. As it was he was to receive the first ever Pathfinder 'badge' – the eagle – posthumously and immortality in the ranks of the Pathfinder 'greats'. Our old friend Basil Robinson resumed temporary command until a replacement CO could be found.

The next few weeks proved to be a quiet time for us, and indeed the squadron. Just after lunch on October 5, we test-flew Halifax W7804 prior to the night's operation, an attack on Aachen. We were screening a sprog flight engineer, according to my log book, so for some reason that probably made sense at the time I volunteered to fly as the mid-upper gunner and see if I could put my gunnery training into practice. It was not a happy experience. The weather over the UK was foul, with heavy thunderstorms. The Pathfinder marking was inconsistent, and most of the bombs intended for the historic city fell instead in a small Dutch town 17 miles away. Worse still, my flight commander, Squadron Leader Jack Kerry DFC and his crew failed to return. Jack was 23. Among those killed was the squadron's replacement gunnery leader, Flight Lieutenant Royston Carrington – the second such section leader to be lost in as many weeks. Kerry was replaced by Squadron Leader Griffiths.

The squadron received visits from a number of distinguished guests during the month, including the C-in-C Bomber Command, Arthur Harris, and His Royal Highness The Maharajah Jan Sahib of Nawangar – the member for India on the Imperial War Council. He was treated to a flight in one of the squadron's Halifaxes. A press photographer from Fox Studios was there and we had all of our aircraft and crews lined up out on the tarmac for inspection, with the groundcrews standing dutifully behind. (One of the photographs that was subsequently published is interesting because it shows a Halifax without guns in its front turret. This was in preparation for its removal as an interim measure to see whether it was responsible for a spate of aircraft crashes.)

The calls on Bomber Command's purse during this time – at least in terms of its resources – were many and varied. The allied invasion of French North Africa – codenamed 'Torch' – was timed for early November, and the bombers were to play a small, but not insignificant, part in the proceedings. Their role was in fact fourfold: dropping leaflets over France to explain the rationale for attacking French-owned colonies; dropping mines in Genoa and Spezia to contain Italian warships; bombing cross-channel targets to occupy German fighters; and the preferred occupation – the mass bombing of the major Italian cities including Milan and Turin – to tie down Italian flak and fighters and prevent their use elsewhere.

The first attack happened on the night of October 22/23, just a few hours after the first ships set sail from Gibraltar at the vanguard of Operation Torch. More than 100 Lancasters successfully bombed Genoa without loss and laying waste to several acres within the town and docks. Genoa was attacked five times more within the next three weeks, destroying Italian morale. On October 24, during the day, 88 Lancasters from 5 Group delivered a daring assault on Milan in daylight, reducing the railway system to chaos. A chance to improve upon the damage was handed to a larger force that evening, where this time I was back to my usual role as flight engineer/second pilot though not with my usual skipper. For that evening's operation I had been chosen by our illustrious commanding officer, Wing Commander Robinson no less, to fly with him and his crew. It was my 21st trip. It was a long flight, upwards of eight hours or more, which although well within our range meant that I had to keep a careful eye on our fuel consumption.

I was busy doing this about half way through the trip when I suddenly heard Robinson's voice in the intercom. He sounded very excited, as though something was wrong, so I scrambled through to the cockpit to find out what was going on. As soon as I arrived, Robinson was pointing out of the window. 'Look,' he cried. 'Mont Blanc. Doesn't it look beautiful in the moonlight?' Being only a sergeant, and he a wing commander, I couldn't really tell him what I thought, but let's just say I wasn't particularly impressed.

Despite this particular incident, and Robinson's elevated status, it is fair to say that I held my commanding officer in high regard. He was quite a distant figure to us in those days, and being of such senior rank we didn't see much of him because of his responsibilities. He was a tough Geordie, from Gateshead, with a broad ginger moustache who had played rugby for North Durham, Durham County and, naturally enough, the RAF. He had a big, booming voice like a sergeant-major on the parade ground and a rather brusque manner that some people found hard to take. Personally I got on very well with him, and always thought he was never as bad as he was painted. Everyone knew that he liked to keep goldfish, for example, and that perhaps sounds a little eccentric, but he also liked to read poetry, especially before an operation.

On our return from Milan, I received some sad news concerning my former commanding officer, Wing Commander Bintley, who had been killed in tragic circumstances. His squadron had been involved in the operation against Genoa but on the way back the weather was such that they got diverted to Holme-on-Spalding Moor. One of the 102 pilots (Flight Sergeant Eddie Berry) came in to land and when he was about half way along the runway his port wing struck the cockpit of a second Halifax, with Bintley at the controls, killing him instantly. Bintley's aircraft, it later transpired, had burst a tyre on landing, and had been unable to clear the runway properly. It was a tragic loss of a very fine officer.

The first two weeks of November proved to be a busy time for flying. I clocked up more than seven hours of night-flying training, consumption tests, and fighter affiliation exercises. On November 9, the target was Hamburg, and not all went according to plan. Thick, icy cloud greeted the bomber force over the target, making the Pathfinder's job virtually impossible, but I had a greater threat to worry about. I was lying between the wing spars changing over the fuel supply when I thought I could smell burning coming from the bomb bay so I took off my oxygen and intercom and went to investigate. I opened the cover to the bomb rack and great clouds of smoke came billowing out. I raced forward, opened the bomb doors and jettisoned the flares and the bombs in double quick time.

At that very moment, our mid-upper gunner shouted to our skipper to corkscrew as he had seen flares bursting underneath his turret and taken them to be a fighter attack. When we got back to base and looked in the bomb bay, the fuse cover which stopped the small arming propeller turning and should have been still attached to the flare when it was jettisoned was instead still attached to the fusing link. This meant it can never have been on properly in the first place, and the propeller had been slowly turning in the bomb bay with the net result that it ultimately 'fused' the flare. The striking pin must have struck the delay fuse which would burn for 40 seconds before it finally exploded. (40 seconds was sufficient to allow a flare to drop from 20,000ft to 3,000ft where it was designed to ignite.) It was this burning that I could smell, which gives you some idea how close we came to total disaster. Another few seconds with the burning going undetected, and the flare would have ignited, almost certainly setting off our main ordinance. It was a lucky escape, acting on my own initiative, without the permission of the captain!

A rather more amusing, but nonetheless potentially dangerous incident occurred to me a few days later, with our crew (in Halifax W7804) having been briefed to attack Turin. I had a particular liking for baked beans, so when beans were on the menu for our pre-flight meal I was delighted. Some of the others in the crew weren't so pleased, so they let me have theirs. Needless to say I was even more full of beans than usual by the time we started flying.

Turin is a long flight – more than seven hours – and required flying over the Alps. Just as we were over the mountains, however, I passed out. No-one knew what was wrong with me and I recovered in time for the bombing run but then shortly after started to get the most excruciating pains in my stomach. The pains got worse as we headed back for base, with the skipper so concerned that he decided to get me down at the first available airfield so that I could get medical attention. The first field we came to was one of the emergency landing strips at Tangmere on the south coast. He got me down and they carted me off to the sick bay. Baked beans, as we all know, can generate an awful build up of wind – especially if you eat too many. Combine a build up of wind with flying at 20,000ft, and you have a serious problem, as I discovered for myself.

I spent the remainder of the day in the sick bay, before another Halifax flown by Squadron Leader Peter Elliott arrived to collect me for the 45-minute trip back to base. I did no further flying for the remainder of the month.

Another squadron pilot, indeed the commanding officer Wing Commander Robinson, perhaps achieved even greater claim to fame that night. Certainly his efforts were slightly more 'heroic' than mine. Taking off from Graveley a little after six in the evening, he was flying with the regular crew of that day's duty pilot, Flight Lieutenant Bobby Plutte DFC – known to most of us as 'Pluto' for obvious reasons. Robbo had successfully reached and bombed the target and had turned for home. What the crew didn't realise, however, was that one of the flares had hung up and was still in the bomb bay. They suddenly found themselves in the position that we might have been in a few night earlier. Smoke started filling the fuselage and Robinson thought the aircraft was on fire. Although he opened the bomb bay doors, all that achieved was to fan the flames even more and so he ordered the crew to bale out. Everyone managed to get out safely and then Robinson decided it was time for him to go too. But as he put on his 'chute, the flames went out. He checked to see if there was anyone else still onboard but he was alone.

Robinson was faced with a difficult choice. Either he could bale out himself, and spend the remainder of the war in captivity, or he could fly the bomber home. This, of course, would have been a difficult enough exercise with a full crew in a damaged aircraft with 700 miles still left to fly, but now Robinson was contemplating making the trip solo. At any moment he could have been intercepted by a nightfighter and would have been defenceless, but miraculously he managed to fly and navigate the Halifax back to the UK where he landed at the first airfield he could identify, switching on all of his lights to make sure they could see what he was going to do.

The airfield was Colerne in Wiltshire. One can only imagine the faces of the ground crews when only the pilot emerged from the heavy bomber. The views of Bobby Plutte, whose crew Robinson had 'borrowed' and not brought back is similarly not recorded! Needless to say Robinson was awarded a bar to his DFC for his night's work.

Christmas at Graveley was a relatively happy affair. Operations in December were few, casualties were zero and the squadron spent most of what little flying time was available undertaking the usual pattern of training. I took a short trip on December 21 with Flight Lieutenant MacKenzie down to my old haunt at Boscombe Down, and flew as rear gunner with the CO up to Kinloss for the New Year celebrations. My log book for the month was duly signed by yet another new officer commanding A Flight, Squadron Leader Ian Brownlie DFC, who confirmed that I had flown a total of 23 sorties (since becoming operational) amounting to a little over 150 flying hours. Brownlie himself was a veteran, having survived a tour with 77 Squadron flying Whitleys in 1940. He was only 22 years of age.

It would be two weeks before I was again called for operations.

*   *   *

Towards the end of 1942 and the start of the New Year there was not a little excitement at Graveley with the installation of a strange series of pipes along the length of the runway. Unbeknownst to most of the crews at the time, this was a FIDO installation, a fog-dispersal experiment that would help bombers land even in the most extreme weather conditions. The science was simple: thousands of gallons of petrol were fed along the tubes and lit; the heat caused the fog to disperse, at least in theory. Graveley was one of the first stations to be thus equipped, and when it was first tested, the resulting smoke and flames caused fire brigades from many miles around to rush to the scene, believing the whole airfield to be on fire! Bennett arrived to test the facility for himself, and left satisfied that it posed his Pathfinder crews no danger; indeed, it could be to their positive advantage.

Two other 'secret' devices were also being trialled that would more directly impact Pathfinder operations. The first was Oboe – a blind bombing device that used a series of 'pulses' transmitted from ground stations in the UK and 'received' by Oboe-equipped aircraft that could identify the precise moment at which bombs should be released to hit the target. The second was H2S (also referred to as 'Y' equipment), an airborne ground-scanning radar that enabled navigators to 'see' the contours of land and water on a cathode ray scope, often with a startling degree of accuracy. Although by no means foolproof, and often prone to faults, the introduction of H2S was an immensely important weapon in the Pathfinder's armoury, and 35 Squadron navigators were among the first to receive training for their new 'sets'.

The U-boat pens at Lorient were the preferred target for the first operation of the New Year with seven aircraft from 35 Squadron involved as part of a larger force of 122 aircraft detailed for the attack on January 14. The briefing was unusual in that it was not just the pens that were to be attacked, but also all of the surrounding area and infrastructure on which the U-boats depended.

As engineer/second pilot in Halifax W7821, I was soon in the thick of it. Our pilot (Malkin) dropped 28 flares and 240 of the small 4lb incendiaries from 11,000ft and then it all started to go wrong. Firstly the instruments (specifically the air speed indicator – ASI) froze up, the gyro compass toppled, and the next thing we knew our rear gunner (Sergeant Fryer) was calling for evasive action, having spotted an Fw190 (a single-engined Focke Wulf fighter) on our starboard beam.

Malkin dived down 600ft in a 45 degree turn in a sort of half corkscrew and then climbed back to our original height and course. The fighter then attacked a second time, and once again the pilot took evasive action. This time, however, our mid-upper gunner, Sergeant Emmerson, managed to get a clear shot at the fighter and put in a two or three second burst. The German then came at us for a third time from the starboard beam and slightly below. All of that fighter affiliation training must have done some good, because Emmerson once again let him have it for about five seconds, and I could clearly see his bullets hit the fighter in the belly. There was a shower of sparks and then the fighter turned away.

Whilst there was no visible damage to our own bomber, a little later into the flight home I was obliged to 'feather' the port outer engine. This was probably less to do with the enemy fighter and more to do with one of the principal problems with the Halifax's oil system at this time. The radiator tended to be very efficient, indeed so efficient that it often cooled the oil down too much in the middle such that it became too viscous and therefore struggled to flow properly around the radiator.

What you had, therefore, was a scenario where the oil at the centre of the radiator was cool, and the hot oil from the engine flowed around the thickened oil in the core (the problem was referred to as 'coring') and back to the engine, having lost none of its heat. The temperature on the engines started to rise, and the only thing you could do if you didn't want the engine to seize up completely was to switch it off, feather the propeller, and wait until the heat had spread more evenly throughout the system and you could try starting the engine again. That sounds fine, but you're having to make these decisions and work out what might be wrong whilst under attack from a fighter, and having the feet kicked out from under you on a regular basis.

Despite our ordeal, the aircraft made it back to base in one piece, albeit that a second engine – the port inner – also cut on landing. A return to Lorient (in Halifax W7887) the next evening and again on January 23 (in a different Halifax again – W7804) passed without incident. Sandwiched in-between was the squadron's first attack on the 'big city', Berlin.

Berlin was not comparable to the Ruhr in terms of its industrial importance, but neither was it a city of mere political significance: it had numerous war industries, notably around precision engineering, motor and electrical works. It was also an inland port, connected via a series of canals and waterways to virtually every part of Germany. It was another long haul – a round trip of about 1,200 miles – and not surprisingly it was heavily defended.

This was an interesting trip, as the history books now tell us that it was the first time that proper 'target indicators' (TIs) – as opposed to flares or makeshift indicators called 'pink pansies' – were used for an all four-engined bomber force. Only Halifaxes and Lancasters took part although it wasn't very successful. Flak, fortunately, was light and I believe only one Lancaster was lost (a Lancaster from 5 Group). We returned on three engines after a trip of seven hours and 40 minutes.

Before January was out, Hank Malkin, who had now become my regular pilot, had been promoted flying officer. It was a cause for double celebration when confirmation of my own commission also arrived. Wally Lashbrook had been the first to suggest that I apply for a commission in the summer of 1942 whilst I was still with 102 Squadron but it wasn't until towards the end of that year that I was called to the Air Ministry for my obligatory interview, to see if I was made of the right 'stuff'.

I had been on ops the night before the morning interview, I

can't remember where, but I do remember arriving a little late, and looking a little dishevelled and tired. The interview panel comprised some very senior officers, most of whom I figured had never seen a shot fired in anger. One of them said to me, quite severely I thought: 'Where were you last night?' So I told him the target. The uncomfortable silence that followed was punctured only by the sound of the officer's ego deflating, and I sailed through the rest of the interview.

I was formally discharged from my service on appointment to a commission and granted an emergency commission as No 50954 Pilot Officer on probation in the General Duties branch of the Royal Air Force on January 19, 1943. I thus became, I believe, the first flight engineer on the squadron to hold officer rank. I also became a married man – marrying as a sergeant and returning from honeymoon as an officer. Hank was my best man and Carl also came to see me do the honours.

Every newly-commissioned officer was given a clothing allowance and the necessary coupons and then given half a day to get into London and go into one of the half a dozen or so shops that had sprung up for the duration. It was in one such shop in Cambridge Circus that I bought one good uniform, a greatcoat, rain coat, Van Heusen shirts, shoes and a tie. I recall I didn't have any cufflinks for my shirt and so had to scrounge a pair from my father.

With my commission also came further elevation in my appointment as a section leader. Each of the 'trades' on a squadron – engineers, bomb aimers, navigators, wireless ops, and gunners – had one of their own, often the most senior or most experienced, as their appointed 'leader'. As engineer leader I had to look after everything and anything that related to 'my' engineers. I had an office, a desk, and a chair, and any information that might affect my section came my way. At a personal level, I would keep a check on them all as individuals and help them if there was a problem. I had a sort of mentoring role: I would check their logs, and make sure that they were being kept accurately, and be there to give advice if it were needed.

My 'office' was also the room where the flight engineers kept their toolkits and I distinctly remember one of them, the one-legged NCO who I had mentioned earlier from 102 Squadron called Parks, who used my office and tools to adjust the clutch in his artificial leg because it kept slipping!

Promotions tended to come quickly in wartime, for obvious reasons, but also because it was accepted as one of the benefits of being a Pathfinder. Squadron Leader Ian Brownlie was shot down on January 17 on his 39th operation to become a prisoner of war, and his place as A Flight commander was taken by Squadron Leader Franklin. After Kerry, Griffiths, and Brownlie, I believe Franklin was my fourth flight commander in five months.

At the beginning of February I learned that Fred Lax had been killed. Fred was one of my good friends from my time as an apprentice (his service number was 573105), and in the same Entry (Entry 37). He was operating on Stirlings with 15 Squadron out of Bourn. Either on the way to or back from Hamburg on the night of February 3/4, his aircraft was stalked and attacked by a nightfighter flown by Hauptmann Wilhelm Dormann of III/NJG1. Seven of the crew successfully baled out to become prisoners of war; Fred, the flight engineer, was killed. I believe he was the first of my contemporaries from Halton to be lost in action.[6]

On February 16 and 19, I bombed Lorient (yet again) and Wilhelmshafen, and for my 30th operation attacked Nuremberg, the city that had become synonymous with the black heart of the national socialist regime. By that time, Hank Malkin had become a flight lieutenant – only two weeks after his elevation to flying officer! I finished the month with a trip to Cologne, returning once again on three engines, something that was becoming a habit.

Engine failures were a constant problem, but there were other dangers. As a flight engineer you were constantly checking your instruments and filling out your log every 15 or 20 minutes. We would record the oil pressures and

---

[6]Fred Lax was buried on February 6 at a graveyard in Oosterbeek. Some time after the war I was contacted by Mrs G.J.H. Oosterhaar MBE who had tended Fred's grave both during the occupation and since. I was delighted to be able to send her a photo of Fred, relaxing on his bunk, during our days at Halton.

temperatures on each of the four engines, as well as the coolant temperatures, but the most important reading was the fuel. The Halifax you were flying could have anything from four to seven fuel tanks in each wing, and it was essential to keep a note of which tanks you might be running.

At night, despite the various different exhaust manifolds that were fitted to shield the glow from nightfighters, you could tell the health of an engine by looking at the colour of the exhaust flames. This actually became very important to us. The perfect colour you were looking for was a good blue. If they changed colour, for example if they started to turn yellow, then there was a good chance that there was an internal water leak that could cause the engine to seize. Our Halifax engines had fixed cylinders that could leak, whereas the American-built Packard Merlin fitted to most Lancasters had cylinder liners with a sliding joint at the lower end which made them less likely to leak liquid. So you kept an eye on the coolant temperature, just in case.

Berlin was once again our target for March 1. My 31st trip, and very nearly my last. It was definitely the one that scared me the most.

The day followed a typical pattern. We flew the usual 15-minute air test earlier in the day, checking the aircraft, guns, radar and wireless equipment in preparation for the night's operation. Unless the weather closed in unnaturally so, the sortie would be 'on'. And it was.

There was nothing unusual about the briefing. It followed its normal pattern. A lifetime away from the earlier briefings and raids that were so hit and miss – often quite literally. The CO got up and did his bit, a sort of general introduction if you like. Then he handed over to the intelligence officer who gave us more of the specifics and all of the latest gen, using maps and coloured markers to show us the route and what Pathfinder techniques we would be using. Then the specialists stepped up and talked about navigation, wind speeds, signals, frequencies and settings, bomb loads, aiming points etc. The gunnery leader said something about the aurora borealis and the northern lights. I don't recall the flight engineers getting much of a look-in!

After the briefing, Malkin talked to the navigator (Carl) to work out the best course to and from the target, and I was consulted about fuel loads and fuel efficiency. Because we were still operating many different versions of the Halifax at that time, fuel loads and consumption were important considerations. Then came the waiting time; we were obviously confined to camp on security grounds so as to avoid the risk of any detail leaking about our operation. We were fed, again, eggs, bacon and chips before picking up our flying kit, parachutes etc. and waiting for the trucks to take us to our aircraft.

Arriving at dispersal, I chatted with our Chiefy and the groundcrews about any technical issues to do with flying the aircraft, and once we were happy, the pilot signed the Form 700 and the aircraft was his.

It was the second time we had been to Berlin. We were to be part of a force of more than 300 bombers – Lancasters, Halifaxes and Stirlings. We didn't have a ritual like others. The occasional pee on the tail wheel but more out of necessity than superstition. Rumour had it that it could rot the rubber of the tyre, and the AM had tried to ban it. Total rubbish of course, but a good story. It might rot the hub! The only ritual I did have later in the war, it you could call it that, was that I tended to carry two revolvers with me, like I was in the Wild West. My father had given me a Webley .32 that had been given to him by a friend who had served in the Black and Tans. I also had my own .38 Smith & Wesson and so carried the pair.

The flight out passed without much happening, but as we approached the target, the flak started coming up and we were hit in the port inner engine. Despite this, and despite also sustaining damage to the rudder control rods, Malkin was able to keep the aircraft sufficiently straight and level long enough to bomb the target.

Then we were coned by searchlights – the big 150cm searchlights that worked hand in glove with the flak – and our pilot immediately tried to shake them loose. We didn't dive as there were too many of them. He corkscrewed, weaved and did everything with that aeroplane to get us out of the lights but without success. Every time we seemed to have succeeded they found us again and this went on for more than 25 minutes, by which time the pilot was exhausted.

In heading for home, however, we found that our DR compass was playing up and had to rely on the magnetic compass. Unfortunately we ended up too far south of track and into another barrage of flak on the edge of the 'Happy Valley' (as the Ruhr was known). A shell exploded close by, sending slithers of red-hot shrapnel into the sky, into our aircraft, and into our mid-upper gunner, Flight Sergeant Fryer. We also began having trouble with a second engine. I kept an eye on the flickering needles of the oil pressure and temperature gauges but in the end had to tell our pilot that I was going to have to shut down the port outer. Luckily, by then, I had been able to restart the port inner, so at least we had three engines.

The raid seemed to last forever, especially that second time we were caught in the flak. I remember us just sitting there, fully illuminated, watching our skipper sweating at the controls, with all hell breaking out around us. At one point we lost all lights in the cockpit. I know we all felt extremely exposed, and the gunners also knew that while we were in a searchlight, the nightfighters could easily see us but we couldn't see them.

The journey home was incredibly hard on the pilot. Ideally you would trim the aircraft and adjust the controls to a position that required the least amount of effort to keep the aircraft level. To trim a Halifax was not as straightforward as it sounds. There were very small controls (tabs) on the trailing edge of the main flying controls (i.e. the ailerons, elevators and rudder). The pilot could adjust these trim tabs by way of twisting a series of small hand-wheels. The Halifax was unusual in that instead of having separate controls for the tabs, the hand-wheel was over a square section of the main control column. The hand-wheel turned a control rod that rotated at the flying control end. This turned a sprocket wheel that in turn operated the trim tabs. The problem was that the control rod was damaged, and being at the back of the tail there was no way we could fix it, and so we couldn't trim the aircraft. It meant that an incredible amount of physical effort was required to fly the 'plane.

Maintaining an accurate course was virtually impossible, and with an injured gunner onboard, we put down at one of the first airfields we could find, Swanton Morley near East Dereham in Norfolk. The landing was a bit of a bumpy one, not helped by the fact that our main landing wheels had been punctured. In the end, Hank did a pretty good job. We were picked up the next morning by our flight commander for the short 20-minute flight home.

It wasn't just me who thought Malkin had put on a good show. He was recognised for his work in getting both his aircraft and the crew safely home with the award of an immediate Bar to his DFC, the citation reading:

> "One night in March, 1943, this officer captained an aircraft detailed to attack Berlin. Whilst over the city the bomber was held in searchlights and subjected to heavy anti-aircraft fire. The rudder controls were severed and one of the port engines was damaged, causing it to fail. Despite this, Flight Lieutenant Malkin skillfully controlled the damaged aircraft and executed a successful attack.
>
> Soon after leaving the target area, efforts to re-start the damaged engine proved successful, but further trouble was encountered. The bomber was again engaged by anti-aircraft fire, which rendered the port outer engine unserviceable. The mid-upper gunner was wounded, while all lights in the cockpit failed. With extreme difficulty height was maintained and, displaying superb airmanship, Flight Lieutenant Malkin flew the damaged bomber to an airfield in this country. This officer displayed great skill, determination and endurance in most difficult circumstances."

Not all of the 35 Squadron crews that night were so fortunate. Squadron Leader Peter Elliott, the pilot who had picked me up after my earlier misadventure with a tin of baked beans was missing. Indeed it later transpired that he had been killed, shot down by Leutnant August Geigner of III/NJG1. Also killed was his flight engineer, 'Pop' Watts, the RNAS veteran who had impressed me so much during my days at Boscombe Down. In the remains of the resulting crash, the Germans also managed to successfully recover an H2S set – the first complete set to fall into enemy hands.

There was little respite for Bomber Command crews in the spring of 1943, the period known at The Battle of the Ruhr. Those of us who had faced death one night were expected to do the same 24 hours later. In the first two weeks of March, I went to Essen (twice), Nuremberg, and Munich, the latter involving flights of nearly eight hours each.

Bomber Command was fortunate during its attack on Essen on the night of March 5/6 that the skies were unusually clear. Pathfinders were able to locate the target accurately, despite the best efforts of the Germans to confuse navigation, even going to the extent of draining a nearby lake, the Baldeney See, in the hope of removing a convenient landmark. As the later crews arrived over the target factory sheds could be seen blazing in the light of colossal fires. Contemporary reports following the raid point to the centre of the target being all-but obliterated and 20% of the built-up area having been totally destroyed. An aggregate of 136,300 square yards was severely damaged, and in the Krupps Works alone, some 53 separate shops had been hit, and up to 50,000 workers made homeless.

Krupps was, and still is, world famous, and at the time was the largest single engineering plant in Germany. We were all aware of its significance in manufacturing flak shells, bombs, torpedo tubes, armour plating, tanks, tractors, crankshafts and goodness knows what else to feed the German war machine. It was also a major manufacturer of locomotive trains, and trains were in increasingly short supply. Just outside Essen, too, was the Goldschmidt AG chemical and metal works, and close by were large hydrogenation plants capable of producing aviation spirit from tar. These were all targets of enormous significance, and by the third attack on Essen in as many weeks the impact on the Germans was catastrophic.

In April I once again had the pleasure of flying operationally with Basil Robinson, now a group captain with the DSO, DFC and AFC, and soon to be appointed station commander of RAF Graveley.

An unsuccessful trip to Pilsen to bomb the Skoda armaments factory on April 16 with Flight Lieutenant Paxton proved an amusing affair. It was quite an uneventful trip. We went over the target, we dropped our bombs and nobody fired back or did any damage or anything. So I put my head down, checked the instruments, and filled in the log sheet. We were clear of the target then, so I peered through the astrodome to have a look at the exhausts, just my usual visual check that they were all the right colour. As I looked out, I said quietly over the intercom: 'Flight engineer to navigator. Navigator, if we are going home why is the Pole star on the port side?' There was a little hush that lasted a good 10 seconds before all hell broke loose. The Pole star on the port side meant that we were going east, and by my reckoning heading east from Czechoslovakia was not the quickest or the best way home. As it was, we landed at Ford after a flight of eight hours and 45 minutes, returning to base the next day.

While the trip to Pilsen had its funny side for me personally, my former mentor and friend Wally Lashbrook wasn't so lucky. Homebound at around 9,000ft they were attacked by a nightfighter that set fire to the port wing and both engines. Luckily, all except one of the gunners, Flying Officer Graham Williams, a recipient of the George Medal for bravery, managed to make it out of the stricken Halifax in one piece, and four – including Lashbrook – managed to evade capture. As a strange quirk, Lashbrook's flight engineer that night, a Flight Sergeant Knight, had been at Halton at exactly the same time as his skipper, sharing consecutive service numbers.

By the end of April, I was fast coming to the end of my first Pathfinder tour, but there were still a few surprises in store. Stettin, the biggest port in the Baltic and the gateway to much vital war traffic with Sweden, was the target for my 40th operation, with Paxton once again in the driving seat. We clocked up my longest flight to date – a trip of more than nine hours and 15 minutes, covering nearly 1,300 miles. This took my total operational flying hours to almost 250.

Not surprisingly, after such a long flight, I was exhausted, but perhaps unusually so. Feeling a little unwell, the MO questioned me at breakfast (the MO was a clever so and so and used to hang around at breakfast for the first signs of weakness) and felt my glands. They were clearly swollen and I had a painful swelling in front of my left ear and quite a little pain down the side of my face. The doctor told me to report to sick quarters. Having been on the go for about 18 hours at this point I insisted on returning to my billet and retrieving my shaving kit before reporting dutifully to the sick bay where on closer inspection the MO told me I had mumps and that I would be transferred to a hospital in Ely. I then had the long wait for a service ambulance to transfer me to Ely where I arrived with two other airmen and was placed immediately in isolation.

The nursing sister started laying down the law but I wasn't really in the mood and also outranked her. She demanded that I had a bath, and I was equally adamant that in my physical state I might fall asleep and drown. The compromise was a wash and straight to bed where I slept fitfully until it was time for my medication. I was prescribed penicillin, one of the early recipients, but the doses were substantial and had to be injected in my backside. When the nurses did it, it hurt like hell; the RAF orderlies, however, were considerably more considerate and could put a syringe in without me even waking up! They were worth their weight in gold.

Finally discharged on May 4 and declared fit, I was given a brief period of leave which I enjoyed before returning to operations again on May 25, this time with Pilot Officer George Herbert, a 21-year-old Londoner. Herbert was an experienced aircraft captain and holder of the Distinguished Flying Medal for his bravery as an NCO pilot with 76 Squadron. I flew two sorties with Herbert: one to Düsseldorf, and the second to Essen. Both were completed without incident. Fortunately I was not flying with Herbert on the night of June 11/12 when he was shot down and killed attacking Münster. Indeed it was a bad night for 35 Squadron when the aircraft of 28-year-old Flight Lieutenant Stanley Howe DFC also failed to return. I was flying with a new skipper, Flight

Sergeant Quigly that evening, and the following night when we attacked Bochum. I was still with Quigly for my 45th trip on June 19, 1943, to the Schneider armaments factory and Breuil steelworks at Le Creusot.

We were told it was going to be bright moonlight and it was. We found the target easily; there was no cloud and little opposition. Because of the conditions we were instructed to return to base at low level (so that the nightfighters would have more difficulty in picking us out against the ground). This we did and as we roared across the French countryside, one of our gunners spotted a train and asked the skipper if he could give it a squirt. Both gunners opened fire and seemed to enjoy themselves. Then as we crossed the coast, Quigly started to climb. No sooner had he done so than we were immediately the target of a flak ship which opened up with everything it had. Not surprisingly we dropped straight back down to sea level and beat a hasty retreat.

Two days later, and Quigly was himself posted as missing, although luckily for me I was not on-board. Quigly's aircraft, Halifax HR848, was one of six 35 Squadron aircraft lost in that single, tragic evening. Although Quigly would later turn up as a POW, 20 others were not so lucky. The skippers missing that night attacking Krefeld included Pilot Officer James Andrews, a 23-year-old Canadian, lost without trace with his entire crew; Flying Officer Michael Clarke, 20, also lost with his whole crew; Flight Lieutenant T H Lane DFC and crew, all of whom were captured; Pilot Officer W H Hickson, a New Zealander, who became a POW but lost two of his crew; and Flight Sergeant Donald Milne, a 22-year-old Australian, who survived a ditching, only to lose his life two weeks later. The chop rate seemed to be increasing.

The pace of change on an operational squadron was such that while I had been away on leave, enjoying my promotion to war substantive flying officer on probation (though acting flight lieutenant), a new commanding officer had been confirmed to succeed Robinson's temporary command: Wing Commander Donald 'Dixie' Dean DFC. Dean, a Londoner, had come to 35 Squadron from an operational training unit (OTU) and at the start of the war had been in the Territorial

Army as a gunnery lieutenant, transferring to the RAF in 1940. In September of that year he had been posted to an army co-operation squadron flying Lysander coastal patrols from Linton-on-Ouse, before moving on to 77 Squadron at Topcliffe at much the same time that I had been posted to 35 in Linton. Dixie was quite a distant sort of man, and perhaps a typical 'pongo', but there was no doubting his bravery. In one of his first ever sorties, as a second pilot, an engine failed on the way back from Bremen and he was forced to ditch. Enemy air activity made immediate rescue difficult, and Dixie spent more than three days in a dinghy in the North Sea before he was finally picked up. It was said that Dean had been personally recruited by Bennett, rather than by the usual channels, so he came to us with the highest credentials. He also came to us with Keith Cresswell, who of course I had also known at 35.

Dean's promotion from squadron leader to wing commander came through in May at the same time Robinson took over as 'groupie'. I had an opportunity of discovering first hand what my new commanding officer was like in the air when on August 9 I flew as engineer/second pilot with him to Mannheim – second in size only to Duisberg as an inland port and thought to contain some of the largest grain mills in Germany. Reports at the time suggested that we didn't do a great deal of damage, the bombing being described as 'scattered'. We also lost one of our Australian pilots, Flight Sergeant Brown, and his crew.

By now, of course, I had officially come to the end of my first tour. Mannheim was my 46th trip. Recognition of that fact, however, came with news that I had been recommended for the DFC. This wasn't a surprise as such. If you stayed alive long enough, you got the medals, it was as simple as that.

Others clearly saw my feat of survival as impressive, the citation to my first award (as promulgated in the *London Gazette* July 13, 1943) acknowledging my operational record up to that point:

"Pilot Officer Stocker is a most capable flight engineer. He has taken part in many sorties against the most important and strongly defended targets in Germany and occupied territory, including raids on Berlin, Hamburg, Milan, Pilsen and Spezia.[7] His sound knowledge has on occasions greatly assisted his captain in making a safe return to base. Pilot Officer Stocker has invariably applied himself to his tasks with enthusiasm and skill."

Medals were, and indeed still are, a cause for controversy, and this was particularly brought home to us whenever we came across our American counterparts. Between 1942 and 1945, the Eighth Air Force awarded just over 500,000 medals to its crews. The majority (around 441,000) of these were Air Medals given to aircrew on completion of more than five individual bomber sorties. The second most popular award was the US Distinguished Flying Cross of which some 45,000 were received. These tended to be for specific acts of gallantry, perhaps for shooting down an enemy aircraft. In fairness, they were a little more discerning when it came to their highest award, the Medal of Honor, their equivalent to our Victoria Cross. Only 14 MoHs were awarded to Eighth Air Force airmen, and only 220 Distinguished Service Crosses. Of the 73,651 Silver Stars given to US forces, only 864 went to US airmen in Britain.

By comparison, the RAF's policy towards decorations was desultory. Not for us a chest full of ribbons. We had no equivalent to the American Air Medal, although officers (such as me) who completed a tour of 30 operations might routinely expect a non-immediate DFC. To this end it came to be seen as a 'survivor's' medal, and its impact was slightly diluted. Only 20,354 DFCs were awarded throughout the RAF and 1,592 'bars'. Enlisted men (i.e. NCOs) would usually receive the equivalent Distinguished Flying Medal, but despite NCOs being greater in number, the amount of DFMs awarded was pathetically small – just over 6,000. It was an excellent example of class prejudice in action. Suffice to say that I can't think of anyone – officer or NCO – who got a medal who

---

[7] I had in fact not been involved in any attacks on Spezia.

didn't really deserve it, but I can think of plenty who did deserve it but were never recognised.

Although officially classed as 'tour expired' and entitled to a rest, I wasn't banging on the adjutant's door asking for a posting, and there was no let up in my flying routine. I might have been posted to an OTU for six months to help 'sprog' flight engineers, as trainees were known, adapt to operational conditions, but as it was I was somehow retained within 35 Squadron where I proceeded to increase my tally of sorties against the major targets of the day. One such target was Milan, but my attempt to bomb the Alfa Romeo works on August 12 came to naught when our aircraft developed a fault and the port outer went u/s (unserviceable) before we had even crossed the French coast. The captain, Flight Sergeant Daniel, did not fancy traversing the Alps with only three engines in good working order so soon into the journey and I had to agree.

On August 14 I spent 40 minutes aloft with a Kiwi pilot, Flight Sergeant Nicholas Matich DFM (and later DSO), practice landing with the new FIDO facility in full burn. Matich had only recently recovered from a rather nasty crash-landing en route to Hamburg. In fact, he was only one minute into the operation when he suffered a total loss of power – a frightening experience at the best of times but even more so with a full load of bombs and fuel. Fortunately my experience with Matich was less dramatic, although still exciting, as all FIDO landings would prove. The pilot would come in on instruments (visibility was usually zero) and then all of a sudden you would see these enormous strips of fire looking for all the world like the valley of the shadow of death. The heat caused a haze, as you would see in the desert or the beach on a hot summer's day, and it made the surrounding area shimmer. For a brief second the aircraft would become momentarily unstable (as a result of the hot air) and then you were down. Practice was fine, but I'm not sure if I would have liked to have used one in anger, especially if my aircraft was damaged. Matich also never got the chance. He was shot down the following month.

(As it happens, from November 1943 to the end of the war

some 2,700 aircraft were 'rescued' by FIDO installations, although the number may have been higher since records are incomplete. At least 10,000 airmen were probably saved as a result.)

Tragedy was to hit the squadron, and Graveley, once more before the summer had ended. With the Battle of the Ruhr over, the first phase of the Battle of Berlin was gradually getting underway. The historic Peenemünde raid, the first where a master bomber had been employed by the Pathfinders to direct an entire raid, had been a considerable success. Now they were turning their attention once again to the 'big city' itself, Berlin, where a master bomber would again be deployed to direct the main force onto the target.

Unfortunately the raid was only partially successful, despite the best efforts of the man in charge, the Canadian Wing Commander Johnny Fauquier (later to command 617 Squadron). Much of the attack fell outside of the city in the surrounding villages, and the German defences were particularly effective. Officially, 56 aircraft were missing – Bomber Command's biggest single loss up to that point. Amongst the missing was Halifax HR928 flown by 29-year-old Flight Lieutenant Harry Webster. Webster's bravery had already been recognised with a DFC. Indeed every one of his crew, with the exception of the flight engineer, held either the DFC or DFM, but he had on-board an even more distinguished co-pilot with a DFC, AFC and a DSO: Group Captain Basil Robinson.

Robinson was in fact one of three station commanders flying that night – men clearly prepared to lead from the front no matter how dangerous the target. The other two were Group Captain 'Press on' Fresson, station commander at RAF Bourn, and the station commander of RAF Oakington, Acting Group Captain Alfred Willetts. Whereas Fresson would make it home, Willetts, like Robinson, was also shot down. Luckily he survived to become a prisoner of war, along with his pilot, the highly-experienced Squadron Leader Charles Lofthouse DFC. Earlier in the war, Willetts had been air adviser to the chief of combined operations. He took part in the successful raid on Vaagso carried out by the three services on December 27,

1941, and was responsible for the organisation of the air plan even flying in the lead Hampden bomber. He was awarded the DSO for his skill and devotion to duty.

Losing Robbo was a big blow, and it so often happened when men like him and Willetts tried to sneak one in. That was why they were so often grounded by the AOC. It may sound a little brutal, but I think we were never surprised when one of the new boys was lost. That was expected. But when someone with real experience went missing, then you began to realise it could happen to anyone. Losing your commanding officer or station commander was a real shaker, and this was a bad night for us because as well as losing Robbo we also lost three other crews – men that we could ill-afford to lose.

Life, however, went on, and on September 8 I had an exciting training sortie with one of the 35 Squadron stalwarts, Flight Lieutenant Julian Sale, when an enemy aircraft in the area put an end to what was an otherwise innocuous flight practicing circuits and landings. Sale was RCAF and had only recently been awarded the Distinguished Service Order for demonstrating 'an unconquerable spirit of determination, great gallantry and fortitude that have set an example beyond praise'. He was to add a Bar to that DSO for a further heroic action in saving one of his crew members before the year was out.

By the end of October, I had accumulated a total of 497 hours and 30 minutes of flying time, 296 of which were in operations. The list of noteworthy pilots happy to have me at their right hand was enhanced immeasurably on the afternoon of October 5, and a visit to the squadron by our AOC, Donald Bennett.

The background to the flight stems from the equipment used by the Pathfinders at that time. Pathfinders had started out operating with four different types of aircraft, and three different types of heavy bomber: the Short Stirling, Handley Page Halifax and the Avro Lancaster. By 1943, Stirling Pathfinder operations had been suspended, leaving the Halifax and the Lancaster to bear the brunt of the attacks. There was logic, however, in rationalising the use of aircraft still further, to make the supply, servicing and maintenance of the aircraft easier, and the training of aircrew and groundcrew alike more efficient. The only issue remaining was which of the two aircraft to choose.

Towards the early winter of 1943, Bennett set about reviewing his equipment policy, to determine once and for all whether his squadrons would use the Lancaster, or the latest Halifax IIIs that were just entering service. Both were fine aircraft. The new Halifax III was powered by the Bristol Hercules radial engines that gave it significantly more power than earlier Merlin-powered models. It had a maximum speed of 312mph, could cruise at 215mph at 20,000ft, and carry 13,000lbs of bombs or munitions. The major downside, as far as I could see, was that it was such a powerful beast that it tended to burn a great deal of petrol in a very short space of time and fuel consumption could be altered greatly if the mixture control was mishandled.

The Lancaster was slower at the top end (maximum speed 287mph), but could carry more bombs a greater distance. With like-for-like loads, the Lancaster's range was some 400 miles further than the Halifax (1,660 miles versus 1,260 miles). Bennett was always a man who made up his own mind, based on his own experience, and so came along to 35 Squadron to try out one of the new Halifax IIIs for himself.

The Halifax flown that day was HX232. Take-off was 15:40, and Bennett spent half an hour putting the Halifax through its paces with just me alongside him. Little mention is made of the incident in Bennett's own autobiography, and subsequent biographers fail to mention the flight at all, but to me it held tremendous significance. There I was minding my own business when a call comes through to my section and I'm told to report to the CO. When I get there I'm told I'm going to fly as engineer leader with the AOC. It was to be his – as well as my – first flight in a Halifax III.

I remember the take-off well because as we pushed the throttles forward, and adjusted for the swing, the aircraft fair thundered along the runway and took to the air with very little effort at all. I was surprised and I know that Bennett was too. It caught us both unawares. That said, there were only the two of us aboard and we didn't have a bomb load or anything like that so the aircraft would have been much lighter than usual.

The flight was only comparatively short which made me think that perhaps Bennett had already made up his mind but needed to put on a show. We played with the undercarriage and flaps (Bennett well remembered the problems with the earlier models of Halifax) and flew a few circuits – nothing too violent. He tested the effectiveness and weight of the controls, with particular emphasis on the rudders (it was a relatively new design) and then declared himself satisfied and we landed. It wasn't much of a trial, but it was enough to decide Bennett once and for all to put his full support behind the Lancaster, rather than the Halifax.

It is interesting to note that Arthur Harris had long before disassociated himself with the Halifax as an effective bombing weapon. Not long after the bomber's introduction he wrote to Air Chief Marshal Sir Wilfred Freeman at the Air Ministry describing the aircraft as a 'virtual failure' that even with proposed structural modifications would still not be fit for the European bombing campaign. As the war progressed, his vitriol became more vicious, and he turned on the new Halifax III specifically. Despite clear improvements in performance, he believed that losses of aircraft and crews 'will ensue on an ever increasing scale if we persist in our present policy of sending crews to fight in inferior aircraft'. He also rounded on Handley Page personally, describing them in a letter to Sir Charles Portal, Chief of Air Staff, 'not as an aircraft manufacturer, just a financier with all that implies and more'.

Harris' motivation was doubtless to get the best aircraft – in his view the Lancaster – in the greatest numbers to his crews in the shortest possible time. That meant transferring production from the Halifax (and the Stirling) over to the Lancaster without delay. Perhaps Harris had made his own views known to Bennett? Doubtless it must have been discussed. Neither men were short of opinions, or held any fear in expressing them. Bennett, however, was very much his own man, and it is difficult to see that he would have dismissed the Halifax III simply because another man told him to do so.

The year was fast drawing to a close. In November, I

clocked up less than five hours training, although I nearly ran into trouble with Squadron Leader Sale on November 3 when we accidentally stumbled into a Luftwaffe air raid on Newmarket, and beat a hasty retreat to observe from the sidelines. On November 15 I spent 40 minutes conducting an air test with a Pilot Officer Everett. This in itself is not significant, other than the fact that the newly-commissioned Danny Everett would later become one of the Pathfinder greats, winning three DFCs before losing his life in March 1945 on his 98th operation.

In December I flew only twice: one of these flights was with a Flying Officer Ken Price on an operation that had to be abandoned when the hydraulics went u/s leaving both the undercarriage and the flaps in the permanent 'down' position. We ended up dropping our bombs 20 minutes after take-off from about 30 or 40 feet – I clearly remember seeing them bounce – and then flying around for the next three hours to lose enough fuel before we could land. The second occasion was with yet another Pathfinder 'great', Pat Daniels.

Daniels had taken over from Dixie Dean the month before – Dixie having left to take up an appointment as CO of Pathfinder NTU. Wing Commander Sydney Patrick Daniels DSO DFC & Bar, to afford him his formal rank and decorations, but universally known as 'Pat', was quite a character. He had joined the RAF as an 18-year-old in September 1940, and had been awarded a DFC on completing a tour of operations with 58 Squadron flying Whitley Vs. He had been an early Pathfinder, starting his second tour of operations with 83 Squadron, and was in fact the first pilot to be officially appointed to a master bomber role, albeit the intended raid against Munich never took place and it was left to Wing Commander 'Honest John' Searby DSO DFC to finally claim the honour. Pat had won a second DFC in November 1942 and added a DSO at the end of his second tour for 'exceptional leadership and outstanding determination'. He was still only 23 when he succeeded Dixie as our new CO, and used to welcome new crews onto the squadron by pointing to an axe above his desk and telling them that they were all for the chop and then compounding the ruse by

Top: Ted in uniform for the first time at just 15. A long and eventful career awaits.

Bottom: RAF Halton: a typical workshop scene with apprentices hard at work, files at the ready.

Top: Halton apprentices later in the war. The variety of wheel types and sizes is worthy of note.

Bottom: Rehearsing on the square for Ted's pa[s]out parade, February 1940.

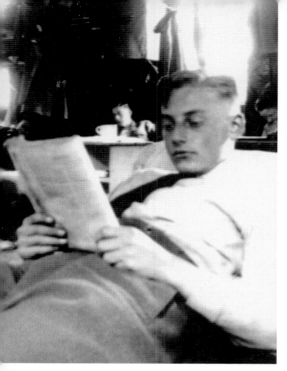

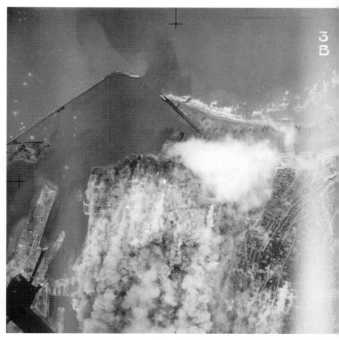

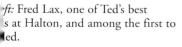

ft: Fred Lax, one of Ted's best
s at Halton, and among the first to
led.

ght: As a corporal air gunner, May
The AG brevet would shortly be
ed by E as Ted became one of the
first flight engineers.

Bottom left: Jimmy Marks, one of the 'greats', and the first to
be awarded the Pathfinder eagle – posthumously.

Bottom right: Le Havre from 13,000ft. Target for the first
Halifax operation of the war.

Top: 35 Squadron, Linton-on-Ouse, September 1941. Basil Robinson is seated (centre) with Leonard Cheshire (8th from left) and Jimmy Marks (9th from right). 'Pop' Watts is second row, second from left (standing) and Ted is 13th from right in the top row.

Bottom: Ted (far left) with his skipper Hank Malkin (third left) and crew in front of the 35 Squadron Halifax 'G' Gre

Middle left: Ted at 21, his flight engineer's brevet, Pathfinder eagle and DFC ribbon clearly visible.

Middle right: 'Dixie' Dean. Succeeded Basil Robinson as commanding officer, 35 Squadron.

Bottom: The groundcrews did not often have the luxury of working inside except for major overhauls.

Top: A good shot of a Halifax in flight and the rudders that caused so much angst.

Middle: Message from the air chief marshal congratulating Ted on the award of his DSO, January 8, 1945.

Bottom: Leonard Cheshire (centre) with his crew including his flight engineer, Paddy (second right) and 'Revs' (far right). Cheshire had a habit of scaring those that flew with him.

Wt. 25617/P. 34 100,000 Pads 9/43 H.P. 51–7341

R.A.F. Form 1924   **POSTAGRAM.** Originator's Reference Num

To: F/L E. E. STOCKER, DFC., (50954),   FC/S.23191/P.
No. 582 Squadron,   Date :—
R.A.F. Station, LITTLE STAUGHTON.   8th January, 1945.

From: The Commander-in-Chief, Bomber Command.

My warmest congratulations on the award

of your Distinguished Service Order.

A.T. Harris
Air Chief Marshal.

Originator's   Time of
Signature   Origin

Top: Keith Cresswell (centre seated), an early 35 Squadron pilot and exceptional Pathfinder.

Middle left: Canadian maestro Julian Sale rode his luck, but it finally gave out.

Middle centre: Squadron Leader Jack Kerry. A Flight commander, 35 Squadron.

quadron crews await royalty. The aircraft (foreground) has clearly had its nose turret 'sealed' whilst porary solution to the Halifax's stability problems is sought.

Top: 'Dipper' Deacon who chalked up more than 100 operations.

Bottom: Cologne – a frequent target – seen from 8,000ft from the Lancaster of a 582 Squadron contemporary and master bomber, George Hall.

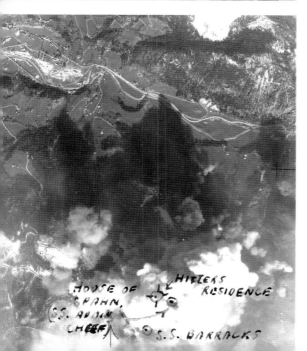

Top left: A graphic image of an unidentified Pathfinder illuminated in the glare of the fires he has helped to create.

Top right: The oil works at Wanne Eickel, October 12, 1944. Ted's DSO citation notes his exemplary performance as master bomber over this target

Middle left: Elmer 'Al' Trotter (third from left) – typified the experience and bravery of Pathfinder crews.

Middle right: 'Hal' Mettam (left) – Ted's pilot for his 100th operation.

Bottom: Hitler's private residence, and a bombing photograph that officially does not exist.

A photographic montage of the cream of Pathfinder aircrew that appeared in an issue of *Flight* magazi[ne] 1945. Ted is fifth from right, bottom row, next to 'Dixie' Dean; above Ted is Peter Cribb flanked by 'Sludge' Collings and Godfrey O'Donovan.

(Below) Group Capt.
R. W. COX,
D.S.O., D.F.C., A.F.C.

(Below) Group Capt.
LAURENCE CHARLES
DEANE,
D.S.O., D.F.C.

Wing Cdr. T. G. JEFFERSON,
D.S.O., A.F.C.

Group Capt. G. F. GRANT,
D.S.O. and Bar, D.F.C.

Wing Cdr.
R. J. BURROUGH,
D.F.C.

(Left)
Sqn. Ldr.
V. G.
ROBSON,
D.F.C. and
Bar.

Group Capt.
K. J. SOMERVILLE,
D.S.O., D.F.C., A.F.C.

Wing Cdr.
ALABASTER,
S.O. and Bar,
F.C. and Bar.

Flt. Lt.
A. PEARSON,
D.S.O., D.F.C.

Sqn. Ldr. J. B. BURT,
D.S.O., D.F.C. and Bar.

Sqn. Ldr. G. W.
O'DONOVAN,
D.S.O., D.F.C.

(Left) Sqn. Ldr.
P. MAINS-SMITH,
D.S.O., D.F.C.

up Capt. P. H. CRIBB,
S.O. and Bar, D.F.C.

(Left) Wing Cdr. R. C. E. LAW,
D.S.O., D.F.C.

Wing Cdr. A. J. L. CRAIG,
D.S.O., D.F.C.

(Above) Wing Cdr.
D. F. E. C. DEAN,
D.S.O., D.F.C. and Bar.

(Left) Flt. Lt.
E. E. STOCKER,
D.S.O., D.F.C.

(Right) Wing Cdr.
H. P. CONNOLLY,
D.F.C. and Bar, A.F.M.

(Above) Wing Cdr. J. R. G.
RALSTON, D.S.O., and Bar,
A.F.C., D.F.M. (Right) Group
Capt. T. G. MAHADDIE,
D.S.O., D.F.C., A.F.C.

Top: Smiling faces with the war at last behind them, May 1945. 582's commanding officer, Stafford Coulson, is centre, with Ted two places to his right.

Middle: Post war engineer officers' course, St Athan 1946. Ted is middle row, second right.

Bottom: The big chief – 'Butch' Harris – at a Bomber Command Association reunion after the war.

Middle: A press call on arrival at Lockheed with Ted in overalls front right, the 'special relationship' very much to the fore.

Bottom left: Pilot at last. Ted has changed his flight engineer's brevet for a pilot's wings.

Bottom right: Alan Craig. Last wartime commander of 156 Squadron and pilot of 'B' Baker.

Top: Contemporary publicity shot of the P2V-5 in flight.

Middle left: Ted shows his VIPs around the RAF's newest aircraft.

Middle right: Lord De L'Isle & Dudley VC and Ted at St Eval, shortly after returning from the US with the first Neptune.

Bottom: (left to right, front, seated) Bill Hough, Jock Calder and Bob Cairns with their Brazilian host (centre back). A time of food and plenty after six years of war.

Walt Muller, USN and crew with 203 Squadron, ~al. Ted is seated right.

Bottom: Ted (third from right) and HQ staff at his final posting, 652 AOP Squadron, May 1956.

Top: Reunion of t[he]
37th Entry of Hal[ton]
apprentices.

Bottom: Ted and [...]
Stocker, Wyton,
August 18, 2002.

exploding with laughter. He was also a good pilot.

When I started keeping a log book, it never occurred to me that anyone would be interested in it later. I did not take much care or note and record any point of interest beyond what the flight commander would want to see when, at the end of the month, he signed it. There was one incident I recall, therefore, that I did not record at the time but have remembered ever since, which happened while we were attacking one of the north German ports.

Just after crossing the coast we were alarmed to hear the sound of four brownings opening up from the rear turret. The skipper was on intercom immediately, demanding to know what on earth was going on. The reply from the rear gunner was slurred, as though he was drunk: "I can see 'em," he was saying, "I can see 'em and I'm going to shoot them all down." The skipper was clearly alarmed and told me to go aft and find out what was wrong.

Taking a small emergency oxygen bottle with me I made my way to the back of the aircraft, and I could see the turret twisting this way and that, from side to side. When it was about in the mid position, I turned off the power supply so that I could then open the turret doors. The gunner was totally oblivious to my presence, operating the controls to no effect. I had changed my oxygen supply to the aircraft system but retained the bottle to give to the gunner. He was still ignoring me so I gave him a little tap on the head with the bottle to get his attention. I then pulled him backwards and connected his oxygen mask to the bottle giving him a direct high pressure supply. I then used the heat from my hands to clear the ice from the valve on his oxygen mask and all was well again.

The explanation was simple, but could have had serious consequences. The type F masks that we were using at the time were prone to freezing with the flap valve open, thereby stopping the economiser valve from operating properly. One of the effects of anoxia (oxygen starvation) is that the sufferer begins to hallucinate and afterwards loses his memory. Indeed after we landed our gunner could not remember firing the guns or being hit over the head.

My time at 35 Squadron and at Graveley had finally come to

an end. Julian Sale, as yet another officer commanding A Flight, signed my log book to attest that I had flown in excess of 205 hours in the day, and 300 hours at night, the majority of which had been on operations.

The New Year signalled a time for change.

CHAPTER FIVE

SURVIVING

By the start of 1944, the Pathfinders had evolved their training regime into a highly proficient – and highly efficient – enterprise. With all due deference to my own skills and those of fellow flight engineers, the essential ingredient to creating a successful Pathfinder crew was the navigator. Bennett had understood this from the outset. The pilot could be the most accomplished flyer, but if he couldn't find his way or be shown his way to the target, his skill was squandered.

New technologies, such as the introduction of H2S, had of course improved matters considerably, but Bennett still required his navigators to be the very best, and that meant additional training. For this purpose, he established the Pathfinder Navigation Training Unit (PFF NTU) and trained navigators to work in pairs. This was one of the fundamental differences between a Pathfinder crew, and a crew from a main force squadron. All Pathfinder 'heavies' carried two navigators: one, known colloquially as 'the plotter', to manage the traditional navigational arts, and the second, known as the 'set operator', to operate H2S.

A further difference was that Bennett required all Pathfinder aircrew to be proficient in two roles, not just the one for which they had originally been trained. Thus it was, for example, that the flight engineer might double as a bomb aimer, as I was shortly to discover.

Even having nearly 50 operations under my belt, I was still expected to pass through PFF NTU, although my stay was unusually short. Arriving at RAF Upwood on January 27 (Upwood was at that time commanded by John Searby, by then a group captain) I flew twice on the same day: a three hour cross-country with Flight Lieutenant Webber and a shorter trip with a Flight Lieutenant Jones handling the controls of a Halifax as flight engineer for the first time.

If you can believe it, this is what I now refer to as my rest period between tours! It didn't last. Such was the casualty rate on some of the Pathfinder squadrons that they scoured the training establishments for experienced aircrew to fill the gaps as quickly as possible. That's why, before scarcely being allowed to catch my breath, I was immediately posted from Upwood to join 7 Squadron at Oakington.

One of the four founding Pathfinder units, 7 Squadron had a justifiably proud tradition. Originally formed at Farnborough, Hampshire, on 1st May 1914, under the command of Major John Salmond (later Marshal of the Royal Air Force Sir John Salmond), 7 Squadron was in action throughout the First World War taking part in the battles of Loos, the Somme and Arras. With the end of hostilities it was disbanded and then reformed again in 1923 as a heavy bomber unit, flying first the Vickers Vimy, then Virginias (the same aircraft I experienced at Boscombe Down), and later the Handley Page Heyfords. In August 1940 it was chosen as the first squadron in Bomber Command to have four-engined bombers, the Short Stirling, and moved to Oakington to commence operations. The first Stirling raid was mounted on February 10, 1941, after which the squadron was constantly in action. In May 1943, as part of PFF, its Stirlings were replaced by Lancasters, with 17 of the squadron's new aircraft taking part on the raid against Peenemünde.

At the time of my arrival, the squadron was commanded by 31-year-old Group Captain Kenneth Rampling. Rampling was typical of those at the very top of their game. He had won the DFC as a wing commander with the squadron at the end of 1943, the citation making mention of a particularly troublesome sortie to Leipzig and his unswerving devotion to duty. He was, in the words of the Air Ministry, an ideal leader.

My first few weeks on the squadron very much mirrored my time at both 102 and 35. Initially I found myself flying with an array of senior officers before being attached to a permanent 'skipper'. I was posted to C Flight, commanded by a Scot,

Squadron Leader Philip Patrick, a true survivor in our eyes for having outlasted a tour of operations on Stirling bombers for which he won a richly deserved DFC.

The one significant difference, however, from earlier squadrons, was that I had to get used to flying a different aircraft: the Lancaster.

I had been able to scramble around a Lancaster on the ground at NTU and read the engineer's notes but never flown in one. There wasn't a huge difference between the Halifax and the Lancaster; if I'm totally honest I thought the Lancaster was far less complicated to the point that I didn't really think you needed a dedicated engineer.

On the Halifax, the job of the flight engineer was an onerous one. In many ways we were considered a 'cheap' co-pilot. On take-off we would sit with the pilot and hold the throttles to prevent them from creeping back and losing power just when we needed it most. Then once we were airborne there was plenty to do. There were levers we had to pull that put a hook on the undercarriage to stop them falling down, and then we had to unhook them when we wanted to land. With the flaps, there was a valve that had to be turned that controlled the flow of oil from the hydraulic accumulator, and this had to be opened or closed depending on whether we wanted the flaps up or lowered. There was a similar device for the bomb doors: you had to isolate them from the supply, but not too early lest you needed to get the bomb doors down in a hurry. And in terms of the fuel, some Halifaxes could have as many as 14 fuel cocks, seven on each side, whereas the Lancaster had just two.

During the war and since, there are those that swear by the Lancaster. Nearly all those who flew it say it was the best. Much of that, however, has to do with the reliability of the Merlin XX engines, and the fact that it never suffered with any design faults with, for example, the rudders. The Halifax had a poor reputation, undeservedly so in my opinion. One thing that nobody could dispute: the Halifax had a better survival rate for crews. Put simply, if you were shot down, it was easier to bale out of a Halifax than a Lancaster, and that is reflected in the figures. I would take that benefit every time.

My first flight in a Lancaster (a Lancaster III) took place on the morning of February 2. Unusually, the aircraft serial number is not recorded in my log book but the pilot is listed as Squadron Leader Richard Campling. Campling was an extremely experienced pilot and flight commander with the DFC who was also recommended for the DSO – an award that was gazetted after his death.

I spent the next 10 days or so in the company of another of the squadron's senior officers, Wing Commander James Tatnall OBE, flying a series of training sorties in Lancaster EE200 (which had arrived at Oakington from 156 Squadron). Tatnall was a reserve officer called up for the duration. He had been appointed squadron leader in March 1940, and a wing commander (war substantive) virtually three years later to the day. He was now with 7 Squadron to gain operational experience, probably before going on to take command of his own unit. This experience usually took the form of what they termed 'second dickey' flights where they paired novice pilots with those with experience of operations by way of a 'soft' introduction to the real thing. It was never that 'soft' of course, and 'second dickey' aircraft were just as prone to being shot down as the rest of us, as Tatnall proved.

I flew with him on the morning of February 15, but was fortunately not in the same aircraft as the wing commander that night when he was shot down and killed, flying as 'second dickey' to one of the squadron specialists, Squadron Leader John Hegman. Hegman was a 40-year-old New Zealander who held the DSO and DFC, and who had apparently told the authorities that he was much younger so that he would not be considered too old for operations.

February 15 proved to be a memorable date for the squadron, in that we lost four of our best crews over Berlin: not only was Tatnall shot down and killed, but so too was Richard Campling, lost with all of his crew – five of whom had been decorated. The other two aircraft missing were flown by Flight Lieutenant Roy Barnes DFC who was killed in action, and Flight Lieutenant Peter Williams DFC who survived as a prisoner of war. Williams had won an immediate DFC for his actions in November 1943 over Berlin, when his elevator controls had been severed by flak, and he had limited control over his aircraft. By skilful flying he was able to bring the aircraft home, but not able to land, and so it was abandoned. Williams had thus taken to his 'chute twice in three months, and survived on both occasions. Overall, however, the survival rate made grim reading: of the 30 men missing that day, 27 were killed and only three made it to reach a prison camp. Some 18 of those 30 had been decorated with either the DFC or DFM, and one held the CGM. Their total 'op' count probably exceeded 800 sorties. These were men that could not be easily replaced.

For me the date was also auspicious because in the 'duty' column of my log book, I have written the initials b/a (i.e. bomb aimer). And in the column marked 'remarks' are the faded words: 'x-country bombing. One bomb'.

On a Pathfinder Lancaster, as I have said, it was different to the rest of Bomber Command. As aircrew we were expected to be able to do two roles: Don Bennett had said, perhaps somewhat disingenuously, that 'any idiot can aim a bomb and drop it so the engineers can do it'. So that was that. We sacrificed a bomb aimer for a second navigator to ensure that we arrived over the target at the right point and at the right time. As soon as we got there, the pilot would say: 'engineer, get down the nose and aim the bombs' – it was as simple as that.

This was a typical innovation from Bennett, a practical 'hands on' AOC with personal experience of operating a bomber and crew. I had been aware of his methods before Pathfinders when he suggested that flight engineers should be able to identify stars useful to navigators. In the Halifax the navigator sat in the nose with very limited vertical vision and would be able to ask the flight engineer if they could see a particular star. At Graveley, in my flight engineer leader's office, I had a planisphere and the engineers had occasional talks given to them by the navigators. I had been grateful for such knowledge on our way back from Pilsen.

My new-found responsibility meant that I began taking more of an interest in the payload. Up until February 1943, the majority of the bombs used had been of the general purpose (GP) type – 40, 250, 500, 1,000, 1,900 and 4,000lbs. The

2,000 and 4,000lb high capacity (HC) bombs were introduced in 1941 and used as aircraft capable of carrying them were made available. The medium capacity (MC) series was designed to replace the GP bombs, which by 1943 had become obsolescent. The first MC munitions of 500lbs, was introduced in mid-1942 with the remainder (1,000, 2,000 and 4,000lbs) in early 1943. The 4lb incendiary, used in the earliest bombing raids, was still in use in 1944 and considered the most efficient weapon of its type. An explosive charge had been added to a small proportion of incendiaries in 1942 as a deterrent to fire fighters, and during 1943 they were incorporated in a cluster projectile to give better trajectory for aiming, and more economical stowage in the bomb bays.

A minute from Lord Cherwell to the prime minister dated September 16, 1943 gives the relative efficiency of these different types of bombs as assessed by photographic investigation of German cities as follows:

Estimated acres of damage per ton of bomb

4lb incendiary	3.25
4,000lb HC	1.5
2,000lb HC	1.25
1,000lb MC	0.75
500lb MC	0.75
1,000lb GP	0.5

It was thus with only minimal training – indeed the dropping of one single bomb – that I next found myself on the Battle Order (February 19, 1944) responsible for dropping five 2,000lb HC bombs onto the target!

My pilot for this first operation in a dual role, and the man destined to be my regular skipper for 26 further sorties, was Flying Officer David Davies. Davies was a rather dour Welshman. He was a Volunteer Reserve officer and good bit older than the rest of us, but nevertheless a damn fine pilot. He was also experienced, having already completed a tour in the Middle East, so I was happy enough that he knew what he was doing.

The red tape on the map revealed by the intelligence officer

at the afternoon briefing stretched to Leipzig, in the east of
Germany, a long haul of seven or more hours that would take
us in over the Dutch coast. One of the cultural capitals of the
Third Reich, with its fine history in book publishing, its choirs
and its cathedrals, Leipzig was nonetheless a legitimate
industrial target. Certain facilities were listed as 'primary
objectives for precise attacks' by the bomber force commanders, among them Erla, an assembly plant for single-engined
fighters and DKF, a manufacturer of ball bearings. As it
happened, the attack proved a most unhappy affair.

We took off at 23:55 in Lancaster JB185 – an old warhorse
that had been on the squadron since September 1943. We were
part of a force comprising more than 800 aircraft, flying in
what they would call later a 'supporter' role. We didn't have
any flares or any job in marking the target, but we were to
saturate the aiming point as soon as possible so that main force
could clearly see where they should drop their bombs. Despite
the diversionary raids, the German controllers were not
distracted, and managed to marshal their aircraft very well so
that we were attacked as soon as we crossed the Dutch coast.
There were running battles all of the way into the target and
out again. The winds, as I understand it, were not as fore-
casted, and so many of the Pathfinders were late which didn't
help. In the end, although we got through unscathed, some 78
aircraft were shot down, including two from our own
squadron.

Of the total that flew, 78 aircraft, 44 Lancasters and 34
Halifaxes were hacked from the skies that night through flak
or fighters, and four lost in collisions while they waited their
chance to bomb. Of our own crews, Squadron Leaders Davis
and Curtis were missing. Kenneth Davis had in fact gone down
with his aircraft, attempting to save one of his crew who had
been injured but could not bale out, and Curtis was reported
as a POW. Both had been attacked by nightfighters.

As well as the two 7 Squadron crews that were lost, my
friend and one-time pilot from 35 Squadron, Julian Sale, was
also shot down and later died of his wounds. Sale was
skippering one of the new Halifax IIIs (that Bennett had
rejected), but after the raid, the casualty rate amongst Halifax

II and V crews was enough to convince the authorities to permanently withdraw both types from further operations against Germany. Harris, who had never been a fan anyway, had finally got his wish.

Two nights later, February 21, I was again on operations to Stuttgart, once more in the company of Flying Officer Davies and 10 x 1,000lb heavy explosive bombs. I then had to wait another two days before I could finally clock up my 50th operation – a seven-hour haul to Schweinfurt. The Germans weren't best impressed with us that night, because we tried a new tactic – splitting our force into two equal parts, separated by a two-hour interval. The idea was simple: to catch as many of the German emergency services out in the open, and so contribute to further destroying their morale. In the event it wasn't as successful as it might have been. I dropped my five 2,000lb high capacity bombs on what I took to be the right place, although post-raid analysis suggests that both phases of the bombing suffered from undershooting and only limited damage was recorded.

We had rather more success the next night in Lancaster ND496 when we attacked Augsburg. The bombing was later described as 'outstandingly successful' in clear weather and against a target with only limited defences. Augsburg had been the target of a famous daylight attack by Lancasters earlier in the war, but this was the first occasion I believe that we had given it our full attention. We were carrying nine 1,000lb medium capacity bombs that contributed to the colossal damage sustained by the town, whose historic centre was completely destroyed. The Germans held Augsburg up as a supreme example of our 'terror bombing'.

March was a busy month, starting with an unremarkable sortie to Stuttgart and then two weeks of training where the accuracy of my bombing is recorded in detail: March 3, four bombs, 96 yards at 5,000ft; March 7, four bombs, 250 yards at 20,000ft; March 15, four bombs, 270 yards at 20,000ft; March 22, three bombs, 80 yards at 20,000ft. For an attack on Frankfurt on the night of March 22, our role as a crew had further evolved from 'supporter' to a 'backer up'.

There were various grades of Pathfinder depending on how

experienced you were and what sort of attack we were undertaking. The master bomber was in charge, usually the most senior or most skilful amongst us whose task it was to control the whole attack. In good conditions, where we could identify the target clearly (usually a visual attack), the illuminators would go in and literally 'light up' the area so that the primary visual marker could go and drop his TIs (they were usually red) as close to the aiming point as possible.

The master bomber would then assess the accuracy of the marking, and if necessary drop different coloured markers (often yellow or green) to 'cancel' the other ones out. Once he was happy that the target was properly marked, he would then call in the main force and tell them what to do. For example he might say 'bomb the red TIs' or perhaps 'bomb 100 yards left of the yellow markers' that sort of thing. Of course after a while the TIs would burn themselves out, or be obliterated by the bombing, so then the master bomber would call more of us to 'back up' and drop further TIs so that the accuracy of the attack was maintained. We all had different roles but the crucial thing was that we all did our jobs properly. That evening our payload included one 4,000lb and two 1,000lb bombs (we always carried bombs) as well as four red TIs to be used at the master bomber's discretion and a mixed bag of incendiaries.

The attack on Frankfurt was a masterstroke of Pathfinder efficiency, a really good example of where we got it completely right. The target was accurately marked and bombed, and half of the city cut off from gas, water or electricity for some time. We returned to base in ND350 in exactly five and a half hours, most satisfied with our night's efforts. Unfortunately, as we gathered for our post-op interrogation – to give our intelligence officers an impression of the raid and what we had seen, it became obvious that something was wrong. Two of our aircraft had failed to return: one piloted by an Australian pilot officer called Hinde of whom nothing had been heard after take-off; and a second skippered by our commanding officer, Kenneth Rampling. Rampling, it would later transpire, was dead, the victim of a nightfighter that set fire to his aircraft as they were approaching the aiming point. Within seconds of ordering his crew to bale out, the aircraft exploded. Three survived to become prisoners of war, the remainder were killed. A Distinguished Service Order for Rampling appeared in the *London Gazette* on April 11 1944, although no mention is made of his passing. It may well have been that at that time he was still posting as missing, and his death had not been confirmed. The Gazette described him as 'a magnificent leader'.

The squadron, however, did not pause for breath. We were on operations again on March 24 to Berlin, and although we did not know it at the time, this was to be the last major assault on the capital. The night was characterised by strong winds, so strong that they carried us and a large number of bombers well south of the target. Some were blown over the Ruhr and the Ruhr defences responded with alacrity. After Leipzig, and the loss of 78 bombers, this raid was almost as bad, with 72 aircraft failing to return, including two from Oakington. Both pilots, an Australian named Thomas Kyle who was 23, and a 25-year-old New Zealander with the DFC named John Mee[8] were among the dead.

Berlin was always an eventful trip for me: in January 1943 I returned on three engines; two months later we came back on three and then lost another on landing. This time round (flying Lancaster JB962) we also had engine failure and it took us well over seven hours to get home.

It was an exhausting trip, and one that was to prove my last with 7 Squadron. A new commanding officer, Wing Commander W. Guy Lockhart DSO DFC & Bar came to replace Rampling the next day. Lockhart, who Bennett himself described as being 'fanatically courageous', would last almost exactly a month before he too was killed, but by that time I was gone.

* * *

The war now was entering its final year, and the demands on the Pathfinders' expertise were growing greater by the week.

---

[8]Mee's elder brother George was lost the following month over Schweinfurt with 57 Squadron.

More aircrew were being trained, and more Pathfinder squadrons were required.

The Pathfinders' order of battle for September 1942 lists four squadrons (excluding a fifth – 109 Squadron – that was retained for experimental purposes) operating four different type of aircraft from four stations:

Graveley	35 Squadron	Halifax
Oakington	7 Squadron	Stirling
Wyton	83 Squadron	Lancaster
Warboys	156 Squadron	Wellington

By December 1943, with its headquarters firmly established in Huntingdon and with formal Group status, the order of battle comprised 10 squadrons:

Graveley	35 Squadron	Halifax
Oakington	7 Squadron	Lancaster
	627 Squadron	Mosquito
Wyton	83 Squadron	Lancaster
	139 Squadron	Mosquito
Bourn	97 Squadron	Lancaster
Warboys	156 Squadron	Lancaster
Gransden Lodge	405 (RCAF) Squadron	Lancaster
Marham	105 Squadron	Mosquito
	109 Squadron	Mosquito

By March 1944, orders were issued for at least two further squadrons to be formed, and for the last remaining Halifax squadron, 35 Squadron, to be re-equipped with the Lancaster. Bomber Command had a pragmatic and effective methodology for creating new squadrons. Most units at that time operated three flights – A, B and C – with each flight led by a flight commander usually in the rank (somewhat confusingly) of squadron leader. To form a new squadron, the authorities simply hived off a flight from an existing squadron to form the nucleus of the new unit. So it was that with effect from March 20, 35 Squadron and 97 Squadron yielded one flight each to become 635 Squadron, and 7 Squadron and 156 Squadron surrendered flights to become 582 Squadron, based in Little Staughton, Bedfordshire.

* * *

I flew into Little Staughton on April 1 with my pilot and crew under the command of our former flight commander, Philip Patrick. Patrick, now with the rank of wing commander, was to be in charge of the new squadron's training regime, and a supernumerary flight commander.

My 'new' flight commander was the New Zealand Squadron Leader Brian McMillan, and the squadron was commanded by Wing Commander Charles Dunnicliffe. Both were experienced men, Dunnicliffe having earlier commanded (albeit for a brief period) 97 Squadron and flown his first sortie as far back as October 1939 whilst I was still at Halton! Whilst these names were not especially familiar to me, I was certainly well acquainted with the station commander, none other than Group Captain 'Fatty' Collings.

When I came to 582 Squadron I was the senior flight engineer, certainly in terms of operational experience, but was not appointed engineer leader. That role, for the first few months until he was shot down, went to Harold Siddons. Siddons had been a Brat on the 38 Entry course immediately after me, and after the war achieved some fame as an actor, playing bit parts in a number of well-known war films including the Dambusters and Angels One Five, but never quite making it as the lead.

There was some 'luck' for us in moving to a new squadron at the time, for it meant that we missed another historical event, but this time one that I was pleased not to be a part of: the massacre at Nuremberg. We had thought that Leipzig and Berlin had been the big chop, but worse was to follow over Nuremberg. Some of the crews that arrived after us at 582 had been on that trip on the night of March 31 and survived, but they were the lucky few. It was Bomber Command's worst night of the war when at least 95 aircraft were shot down, including 64 Lancasters, three from our old squadron and three also from C Flight of 156 Squadron who would have joined us at Little Staughton. It was a sobering thought.

It was not something we dwelt on for any period of time, however. The squadron was operational within a few days, and my first trip came on April 12, part of a relatively small attacking force of 341 Lancasters and 11 Mosquitoes sent to bomb Aachen, the former capital of the Carolingian empire. It passed off without incident, and our aircraft, JB155 returned with all four engines running.

My entry for April 18 is again interesting because of the historical context. It reads: 'Ops. PFF, Base. Noissy (*sic*) Le Sec (Paris). Base. 10 x 1,000MC, 4 x TIs green.' That in itself is not exceptional. But the fact that the operation only counted as one third of a trip, is. The explanation is a simple one, but controversial both at the time and subsequently.

There had always been debate and some disagreement amongst the Air Staff as to how to determine a tour of operations. As mentioned earlier, at a meeting in January 1940 it had been decided that a tour for an aircrewman in Bomber Command would comprise 30 sorties not exceeding 200 hours operational flying. An Air Ministry letter of May 8, 1943 confirms that a Bomber Command tour was 30 trips, and a second tour 20, the only exception being Pathfinders who signed up to a single continuous tour of 45 sorties. The notion of operational 'hours' at this point, however, had disappeared. It was the trips that counted.

These decisions, however, had been based on the premise of a 'typical' sortie lasting circa five hours. As the war had progressed, new targets had come into Harris' sights, and he was obliged to commit a large part of his force to softening up German resistance prior to the invasion of Europe, as well as contributing to the charade of the invasion taking place in the Pas de Calais. Closer targets of this kind meant that the typical average sortie was now much shorter, and crews could be out and back in a little over three hours. Logic suggested that less time spent over enemy territory meant fewer risks to the crews concerned. This in turn led to an order that short trips to France should not count as a 'full' operation. Indeed they should not even count as a 'half' but rather one third of a full trip. Put another way, one trip to Berlin was the equivalent of three trips to France. Conceivably, following the logic to its conclusion, and assuming the majority of a crew's targets were in France, a Bomber Command tour could comprise anything up to 90 trips!

Needless to say, the majority of the main force crews were up in arms at the prospect. Aircraft were still being lost and aircrew killed. My view, however, would not have been a popular one at the time or even now. The fact is that these trips to northern France were easier and far less hazardous than the long hauls to Berlin or the operations to the Ruhr Valley. How can you compare an operation to Somain, for example, that I flew later that month in April that took three hours to one of my earlier nine-hour hauls to Pilsen? They just do not compare.

Maybe I had a different perspective than many. I had been operating since 1941, so to many of them I was a walking miracle. I had survived. But the point was that the whole scale of operations had changed. Now Harris was committing aircraft in numbers that we couldn't possibly have imagined three years previously. Now a raid comprising two or three hundred aircraft was considered 'small', whereas at the beginning if we had that sort of number in the air at any one time it would have been a major raid.

My first op to Essen in October 1941 involved 78 aircraft; the raid on Essen on April 26 1944 comprised nearly 500 aircraft, and that same evening Harris was able to send 200 Lancasters to Schweinfurt and a further 200 Halifaxes and Lancasters to Villeneuve-St-Georges – all in the one night. Of course there were still casualties, but then there were that many more aircraft in the sky to have a go at.

Throughout April, I flew seven trips, and the squadron suffered its first casualties. On April 22, I was part of a force split between Laon and Düsseldorf. We returned safely, but the Lancaster of Flight Sergeant Bernard Wallis failed to come back. In May, we flew four, and Davies was promoted flight lieutenant.

Looking back today, it is fascinating how my log book reveals how close we were to the invasion. The targets of Somain, Nantes and Louvain interspersed amongst more familiar names of Cologne, Essen and Aachen as Harris tried to balance his obligations to the supreme commanders with his own preferred choice of bombing major towns. It is interesting also, given my views that the war by 1944 was considerably less hazardous than it had been two years previously, that we still suffered significant casualties, and lost some very fine men. After Bernard Wallis had been shot down in April we lost four experienced skippers the following month: Charles O'Neill and Freddie Bertelsen (ex 7 Squadron like me), shot down over Montdidier; Stuart 'Sam' Little DFC, killed over Aachen; and Harold Heney, killed over Rennes. Heney had the DSO, and we could ill-afford to lose men of his calibre. None of these men, however, were shot down over what I would consider to be 'dangerous' targets. Such are the fortunes of war. Perhaps the main force crews had a point after all?

On May 9 I had a welcome distraction from operations when I had the honour of being invited to Buckingham Palace to meet the King, and receive the DFC that I had been awarded some 10 months earlier. I remember little of the ceremony itself, other than the hooks that were attached to our breast pocket so that the medal could be easily pinned to our chests, and the instructions not to shake His Majesty's hand too hard and to take a step backwards before bowing. It was tremendously exciting: the King said a few kind words and I thanked him, and then it was all over. My wife and mother, who had both come along with me to the ceremony, were particularly proud, and then we went outside and posed for photographs. That was my first – but not last – brush with royalty.

D-Day, June 6 arrived at last. We weren't operating; indeed I was on leave in Brighton, staying at the Grand Hotel as a guest of Lord Nuffield who was a notable benefactor to aircrew personnel. A number of crews from 582 were operating, however, and briefed to take out various coastal batteries that might hamper the invasion attempts along the French coast. Again we lost another distinguished airman – Squadron Leader Arthur Raybould DSO DFM – shot down on his 79th operation. Flying with Raybould was our bombing leader, Arthur Feeley DFC, an ex-83 Squadron type, as well as three other aircrew who held either the DFC or DFM. His was no novice crew, and to be lost on such an innocuous target gave us all food for thought.

Although not chosen to fly that day – it was the last day of my leave – the following day, June 7, we found ourselves in charge of the attack on the airfield at Laval, home to one of the Luftwaffe's crack fighter/bomber groups, III/SG4 under the command of Major Gerhard Weyart. The Gruppe had converted from the Me109 to the Fw190 in the summer of 1942. Weyart had had a torrid time of it lately, being shunted from one airfield to the next often at very short notice, and losing several of his pilots to marauding Mustangs whilst in transit. The last of his aircraft had arrived at Laval on June 6, albeit that two had been shot down whilst trying to land. Bad weather had limited the Gruppe's operations, and on 9th the Kommandeur himself had to make a forced-landing near Falaise. Now he was back at base, probably wishing he wasn't.

We took off at 00:50 and arrived over the airfield shortly before 02:50 and immediately set to work. Davies was the designated master bomber, and having identified the target both visually (we could clearly see the woods and the road north east of the airfield) and by the green and red TIs that had already been placed by the deputy, we went in for our own run. Davies had rather a broad Welsh accent, and it was left to me to issue the orders to main force as to where to bomb. We were down at about 3,000ft, well in range of the light flak, but we needed to be that low to ensure we hit the target and so I gave the instruction to main force to come down below the cloud so they could be sure of their aim.

I had seen the first of the green TIs fall and could see them burning in the middle of the airfield. I could also see the red TIs burning slightly to the north west. We therefore approached the target with the wood slightly to our starboard and dropped our yellow TIs and bombs (even as master bomber we still carried eight 500 pounders) across the road along the north east edge of the base, by the aircraft dispersals. I continued my transmissions but main force seemed to be stubbornly ignoring my instructions; I couldn't get them to come down. Yes there was a little light flak but not enough to trouble anyone that much.

The failure of the main force to obey instructions was not unusual, but it was intensely frustrating, and it meant that the raid was not as effective as it might have been. Many were distracted by the fires that were burning close to the woods, and the temptation to undershoot (i.e. drop their bombs too early as opposed to overshoot when they dropped their bombs too late) meant several of their bombs fell on the town rather than the airfield, and many more were scattered harmlessly in the open countryside. It had been far from a successful encounter, although for Davies and me – in our first operation as master bomber – several invaluable lessons had been learned.

My 69th trip, an operation to Lens, was characterised by the now familiar, though a little tedious, return on three engines. Coutrolle was the target for my 70th op on June 24, another short haul to northern France to attack a flying bomb site.

Further similar duties were completed on 28th (Blainville sur L'eau) and 30th (Villers Bocage). The former was significant as we lost one of our best captains, 'Splinter' Spierenberg. Splinter was Dutch, and had originally been a merchant seaman, but got rather fed up with sailing after he had been torpedoed twice! He had joined 582 Squadron from 115 (part of 3 Group) and was an experienced operator. Fortunately, Splinter survived the war, but three of his crew were not so lucky.

The second raid was significant because it is when green ink appears in my log book for the first time. Standard practice required us to write in red ink for night-time operations, and green for those conducted in the day. Although my first daylight operation, it was by no means my last. Indeed the pattern of operations from June onwards began to take a new turn, with daylight sorties becoming more prevalent than night-time raids, such was the Allies' air superiority at this time and ability to quite literally swamp the German defences. Ironically, the first heavy bombers had been designed with daylight operations in mind, but had been slaughtered; now we were attacking with virtual impunity.

Accuracy of the attacks was becoming increasingly assured both because of the skill of the crews and the advent of new technologies such as Oboe. Oboe was used ordinarily by the Mosquito airmen who usually shared each Lancaster base. In our case we were teamed with 109 Squadron, which by the summer of 1944 was commanded by George Grant. With his gaunt features and sunken jowls, Grant did not look like the typical 'boys own' vision of an RAF hero but he was incredibly brave, with both the DSO and DFC to prove it (he would later add a Bar to his DFC in 1945). A 28-year-old from Ottawa, he had sailed from Montreal in the spring of 1939 determined to become an RAF pilot and duly received a short service commission. He first served in a Coastal Command squadron (612) flying Ansons on dreary North Sea patrols from Dyce in Scotland, before playing a key role in the hazardous exercise of flying down enemy radio beams in order to trace their points of origin in France and Germany. This Blind Approach Training and Development Unit (a good cover but a complete misnomer since they were actually developing blind bombing technologies) at Boscombe Down resulted in the formation (later) of 109, and it was appropriate therefore that Grant should one day return as its commanding officer.

Oboe was always designed, as far as we were concerned, to be used at night, and by fast bombers such as the Mosquito. Now the powers that be were experimenting not only with using Oboe during the day, but also on heavy bombers, and specifically our Lancasters. Known as 'Heavy Oboe' for obvious reasons, it did not have the overwhelming support of the crews and for very good reason.

In a Heavy Oboe, the Lancaster pilots and navigators flew in the same aircraft as their Mosquito colleagues, but were effectively glorified taxi drivers. The 582 Squadron pilot would fly the aircraft to the target, and then swap with the 109 Squadron pilot for the actual 'run'. There was also usually a back-up Oboe-equipped Mosquito to take over just in case. We were then in their hands. The diabolical thing is that whilst he is on the run, there is no intercom, nothing, just a deathly hush. You have earphones but cannot hear; a microphone but cannot speak. Oboe was officially known as a 'PD' or precision device and for the device to work you had to fly at a set height and a set speed for a specific period of time (anything up to 10 minutes). That's all very well but if you can imagine being sat there, flying straight and level with people firing guns at you, not able to warn anyone, and just hoping that nothing hits you until the bombs are released, its clear why these operations weren't popular. I think the boys in the Mosquitoes had a better deal with Oboe because they were a lot higher up, but in Lancasters, Oboe was no fun at all.

I had the honour, if that is the right word, of being chosen to take part in the very first of these Heavy Oboe experiments on July 14. The target was a V1 construction site – St Philiberte Ferme. Davies was to play taxi driver with our usual navigating team of Flight Lieutenants Guy and Anstey, before handing over the controls to Flight Lieutenant Charles Grant and his navigator Flying Officer Harold Boyd. We took off at 14:45, and when we were about 15 minutes from the target we had the performance of Grant swapping seats with Davies and his navigator clipping on his headset to listen to the strange warbling noise and the signal to release his bombs. Not surprisingly, the precision device started to play up, and although we should have been accompanied by a reserve Mosquito just for this very eventu-ality, the Mosquito had failed to show. Grant was forced to abort the attack and in the end one of our other pilots (Flight Lieutenant Clive Walker) had to take over the attack and make the best of it. It wasn't a great success and I had to write DNCO (duty not carried out) in my log book. It still counted as an op, however.

My last flight with Davies was to Lisieux, an eventful trip in that the nav two (Norman Anstey DFM) was slightly wounded. Anstey had won his DFM whilst still an NCO flying with 149 Squadron back in July 1940, and was already flying on borrowed time. Within days, Davies, and the nav one Flight Lieutenant Guy, had left the squadron. This wasn't a surprise; Davies always seemed to be in a hurry. He was in a hurry to finish his tour and in a hurry to move out of the squadron. I don't even remember him saying good-bye, I just remember he and his navigator came as a pair, kept together, and then left as a pair. Davies was awarded a DFC in September for his work whilst at 582 Squadron, and added a DSO by the end of the war for his time at 139 Squadron, part of the Light Night Striking Force (LNSF). He will have earned it.

Without a permanent skipper, I found myself a 'spare bod' – literally an 'out of work' specialist who would make up a crew if the regular engineer was missing. I didn't mind, however, because by this time the squadron had a new commanding officer, my old friend Peter Cribb.

I had first got to know Cribb when we were at Linton on 35 Squadron. We were in the same flight, but it wasn't until we got to Graveley that we actually became friends. He had been operational since 1940, taking part in the ill-fated Norwegian campaign. He completed his first tour by June 1941 and then returned to operations in early 1942 becoming one of 35 Squadron's most respected flight commanders. By November 1942 he had already passed 50 sorties and been recommended for the DFC (by Jimmy Marks) quickly followed by the DSO.

It is difficult to remember how we became close – or as close as war would allow. War did that to you. I do remember that there used to be a competition to see how many people he could cram into his car before we set off for one of our many booze cruises, usually to the Ferry Boat Inn in St Ives, a favourite haunt for Pathfinders in the surrounding area.

Cribb was Oxbridge and then Cranwell educated and very bright. (After the war he lectured in nuclear physics.) His family was from Bradford, and I believe had made their money in wool. I stayed with them on one occasion (we flew up to Yeadon airfield – now Leeds Bradford Airport) and they made me feel most welcome. It was on his instigation that I got myself a station motorbike and would nip over to the American airbases and borrow their films, thus fulfilling my obligations as the squadron's one-time 'entertainments officer'.

With Peter's arrival, I began to be more directly involved with the selection of crews for operations, and in overseeing the training of others within my 'trade'. On Pathfinders, most of the flight engineers – indeed most of the aircrew generally – were very experienced and very capable, so there wasn't that much to do. When Peter joined us as CO, I would often be consulted along with the adjutant ('Timber' Woods) and flight commanders as to who would be flying that day.

Putting together the 'Battle Order', as it was called, was horses for courses; the trick was in picking the right horses. We had two flights, and unlike a main force squadron these flights were distinguished by being either 'blind' or 'visual' bombing experts. Determining the Battle Order, therefore, was in a large part determined by the duty required, and the expected conditions over the target. Then we would look at what operational skills were needed, and what specialists we had – for example visual primary markers, illuminators etc. Pathfinders were 'promoted' through experience to take on the more demanding roles, and if we saw an opportunity for a crew to climb one more step up the ladder then we would take it. There were also other factors we would consider: for example if a crew or individual was about to go on leave (the rule was six days off every six weeks served – although with the casualty rate it was never quite as simple as that) then that would be taken into account; if a crew member was sick we were also disinclined to break up a working team, especially if it was one of the navigators that was poorly. Wherever possible we kept the crews together. It was rarely the preferred option to have a crew fly with a spare bod.

Having said that, over the next few months, I flew as spare bod with some of the squadron's most experienced pilots: Bill Spooner (to Bremen), John Goddard (Stettin), Clyde Magee (Wilhemshafen), and Reg Hockly DFM (Düsseldorf). During that time we took more casualties. In July we lost two crews: one skippered by Raymond Rember, an American from Cincinnati, and a second by Squadron Leader Coleman. He was the only survivor. August was especially grim. The aircraft of Squadron Leader Bob Wareing DFC & Bar was shot down on the night of August 7/8; five nights later, Flight Lieutenant Elmer 'Al' Trotter DFC, DFM was also lost, although Trotter survived to become a POW. He had won a DFM on his fourth operation when with 101 Squadron, having brought his badly-damaged Lancaster home against the odds. He was later to endure interrogation in the hands of an enemy intent on his execution, before being 'released' to months of hardship in a prisoner of war camp.

August ended with the loss of yet another aircraft, and this one was felt particularly keenly by our commanding officer. The Lancaster in question was piloted by an Australian Squadron Leader Allan Farrington; the flight engineer, nav one, nav two, wireless operator, and two air gunners were the regular crew of Peter Cribb, and had arrived at the same time as Peter from Graveley. Because of the rules forbidding senior officers from flying all but the occasional sortie, Cribb was obliged to surrender his crew to others to complete their tours. Despite Farrington's undoubted experience (he had fought in Greece and Libya) and skill as a flying instructor (he had commanded one of the RAF's flying training schools at Little Rissington), they were tracked by a nightfighter, shot down and killed.

On September 4 I was once again paired with the AOC, Air Vice-Marshal Donald Bennett. Bennett came to 582 Squadron because he was needed for a conference in Le Bourget. By now the invasion had been a success and the Allies were beginning to move inland at some pace. Eisenhower, the Supreme Commander of Allied Forces, was hosting a meeting and Bennett was obliged to attend. It was only a two-hour trip from Little Staughton to Le Bourget, although we were in no rush. We got there around two o'clock in the afternoon. I had some time to kill and decided to seek out a little bistro nearby. I ordered a glass of wine but before I could drink any, somebody started shooting at us. I decided at that point not to hang around!

We returned to Staughton late in the afternoon of the 4th, and found I was again on the Battle Order for the next day to fly with Peter as master bomber. It was to be my 80th trip, and the target was Le Havre.

Le Havre was one of the pockets of troop concentrations along the coast that the Allies had left behind them during their advance through France, Belgium and Holland. These garrisons, including Le Havre, had been ordered by the Führer to hold out to the last man and so deny the Allies use of essential harbour facilities for landing further supplies. Le Havre was under the command of Oberst Eberhard Wildermuth who in civilian life had apparently been a bank manager. I don't know how much money he had on him at the time but we know he had plenty of troops and munitions at his disposal, including more than 11,000 men and 115 guns. The task of breaking their morale was left to Bomber Command, and we dropped more than 9,500 tons of bombs in seven days.

The attack on September 5 was the first of these runs, involving 348 aircraft in all. We took off in the late afternoon/ early evening, just after 6:00p.m. for the short hop across the water to the target, arriving just less than an hour and a half later. Peter quickly sized up the accuracy of the TIs and instructed main force to overshoot by two seconds. Our deputy then promptly put his TIs precisely on the aiming point and Cribb amended his instructions accordingly. The bombing appeared to be well concentrated and a good number of fires had started just where we wanted them, without the outlaying suburbs of the town being touched. No aircraft were lost.

This most satisfactory expedition was repeated the next day with a similar number of aircraft and with ours (PP149) as the master bomber. Although there was some overshooting into a neighbouring village early in the raid, the vast majority of the bombs – including our own six 1,000 pounders – fell in a rough circle 800 yards across. We were home within two hours, and again there were no missing aircraft.

For the attack on the 8th I had a different pilot, Freddie Gipson DFC, and a different role, as a backer up. Gipson was a volunteer reserve officer who only a few months previously had been a flight sergeant and was now an acting flight lieutenant. The attack was most eventful, especially in our aircraft. The target was largely obscured by cloud and so Freddie brought us down to below 2,500ft for our attack. The first time around we came across the aiming point too late and I was not able to mark. Flying in again I dropped my red TIs and had the satisfaction of seeing one land directly on the aiming point, and the others fall about 100 yards to the south east. Then the flak started to come up at us and the pilot was forced to take evasive action. This had the result of toppling the bomb sight gyro and so we decided to hang on to our bombs and head for home.

The attack on the 8th was significant, not because of the success of the operation – indeed it was all-but a failure with only a third of the attacking force able to bomb – but rather because it signalled the end once and for all for Stirlings in a bombing role. It also signalled the end for our own Flight Lieutenant John Goddard DFC with whom I had operated on a nine-hour trip to

Stettin less than two weeks previously. He was 21.

By the beginning of October 1944, my total flying time had exceeded 300 daylight hours, and 450 at night. September had ended with three more short hauls to Holland and northern France, the first with Peter Cribb as master bomber to The Hague; the second with Squadron Leader Wilfred 'Bill' Spooner DFC & Bar as deputy master bomber to Cap Gris Nez; and the third with Flight Lieutenant Godfrey O'Donovan to Calais.

I think at this point it is worth telling you something about Godfrey O'Donovan who was a most remarkable character. Known universally either as 'OD' or 'GOD', because of his initials, the nicknames were not necessarily meant to be flattering. Some wondered if Godfrey thought himself divine – certainly his all-NCO crew appeared to think so. They seemed to worship him and would take to calling him 'sir' at all times whether flying or on the ground – never skipper or skip, only sir. I flew with him on a few occasions and there was no doubting his ability as a Pathfinder, but his flying skills certainly gave others cause for concern.

When he arrived at 582 Squadron he had already put up a tremendous 'black' by misjudging his height and clipping an aircraft hangar. He did the same while he was with us, taking off the wrong way down the runway (i.e. taking the shortest route) and clipping a church steeple as he cleared the airfield perimeter. He damaged the undercarriage so badly he had to carry on to the emergency field at Woodbridge. There was a court of enquiry and I believe they put it down to being rather flak happy. Perhaps we all were.

Arguably my most memorable trip was still to come, when on October 3, 1944 I could claim to have been the man who broke the dyke at Westkapelle.

Westkapelle was the most western point of the island of Walcheren, the island that effectively held the key to the use of the port of Antwerp, which in turn held the key to the Allies' success in Northern Europe. Antwerp could handle more that 40,000 tons per day of urgently needed supplies, assuming the cargo vessels could negotiate the heavy coastal batteries on Walcheren that threatened to sink them. The navy called in the

RAF, and the RAF called in the Pathfinders.

The plan was for an attack by eight waves of bombers, with 30 aircraft to each wave. Initial marking was by Mosquitoes, with the crews of Peter Cribb, Wing Commander Dickie Walbourn, Flight Lieutenant Godfrey O'Donovan, and Squadron Leader Bill Spooner – four of the most expert of all experts on 582 Squadron at that time – in charge of the show. Cribb, as was usual during this period, was master bomber, and asked me to accompany him as flight engineer/bomb aimer.

We were flying in ND750, a BIII. It was a daylight raid, take-off at 11:55, and our brief was to bomb the island of Walcheren on the Scheldt Estuary. The idea was to make the island uninhabitable for the Germans by knocking a hole in the sea wall. It wasn't a big raid as far as aircraft were concerned, but that doesn't mean it was over with quickly. As it happened we stayed over the target for a couple of hours and they were sending in 30 main force aircraft every 20 minutes or so.

The attack started well, the first TIs going down at 12:57 (zero minus 3). A succession of 1,000 and 4,000lb bombs hit the target over the course of the raid, causing a breach 100 yards across, and all of a sudden the seawater came flooding in. Peter had been controlling the raid, issuing instructions, but the best bit of all was still to come. Out to sea there were eight Lancasters from 617 Squadron, the Dambusters, waiting to be called in if the main force aircraft failed in their task. The Dambusters were carrying massive 12,000lb bombs, nicknamed 'Tallboys' that had the effect of creating a miniature earthquake. Of course it was well documented that 8 Group and 5 Group were intense rivals, and their respective commanding officers – Bennett and Cochrane – disliked each other enormously. The joy we had, therefore, in calling up the Dambuster leader and telling him that their 'special' weapons would not be needed and that we could manage without them gave me considerable pleasure. We all agreed it was one up for Pathfinders.

There was only one anti-aircraft emplacement at West-kapelle, if I remember correctly, right on the tip of the island and earlier – between I think the first and second wave – I lobbed a few smaller bombs in their general direction. We had the joy of seeing the brave Hun get on their bicycles and cycle down the main road straight through the middle of Walcheren Island to the mainland. Seeing the Germans doing a runner was satisfying indeed.

After the fun at Westkapelle, I had leave owing to me and was not on operations again until October 12. The war had now entered yet another 'phase'. A list had been drawn up of targets that would disrupt the Germans' oil production and supply, with names and places appearing on the teleprinters from Group that were not especially familiar to us such as Nordstern, Scholven, Wesseling, Homburg, Sterkrade and Leuna. A further name, Wanne Eickel, also appeared, and would be the target for yet another daylight sortie as master bomber.

For 582 Squadron, it was quite a big affair, putting up 10 out of the total of 111 Halifaxes and 26 Lancasters of 6 and 8 Groups. I was flying with master bomber Peter Cribb in Lancaster PG238 for what was an early morning show, taking off with a bellyful of TIs and just the two 1,000lb bombs. I was the flight engineer/bomb aimer, and was able to confirm the aiming point quite clearly as the canal, the docks and marshalling yards and the triangle formed by the railways was perfectly visible. Wing Commander Brian McMillan was with us as deputy, and we exchanged details of wind speed and direction before the first of the red TIs went down. The target was accurately marked, as far as I was concerned, and clear instructions were issued to bomb the near edge of the TIs. Very soon afterwards, the target began to be obscured by smoke, and but for only the briefest moments, the TIs were almost impossible to see. Thick white smoke with a blue trail was very much in evidence, and I could see the occasional bright orange flash beneath it as another bomb found its mark. There was quite a proportion of main force that were late over the target, but overall we were satisfied with our morning's work and after 10 minutes or so of issuing instructions we headed for home, landing back at Little Staughton just after midday.

I was happy with how the raid went, but notice that a post-war analysis of the attack (quoted in *The Bomber Command*

War Diaries) states that the refinery itself was not seriously damaged but that the GAVEG chemical factory was destroyed. It reads: *'It is possible that the bombers were aiming at the wrong target!'*

I can only say, with some degree of certainty, that I was most definitely aiming at the *right* target. What followed afterwards – and remembering that much of the main force was late – may be the reason why others think we were mistaken after the event.

Wanne Eickel was my 87th operation; for my 88th I flew with a Torontonian, Clyde Magee who – I was interested to learn – had originally enlisted as an air gunner, so we immediately had something in common. Magee was one of the squadron 'originals' who had had the honour of dropping 582's first bombs in anger. Our trip, a short jaunt to Wilhelmshafen, passed without incident. (According to the 582 Squadron ORB, the flight engineer was Flight Sergeant L. I. Walker.)

A most intriguing few lines in my log book for November 23 suggests a 10 minute flight to Wyton and back and a 50 minute sortie with Peter (by now a group captain) to test a new smoke generator. It was an experiment that almost had disastrous consequences. Someone had come up with the idea of attaching a smoke generator to the bomb bay of a Lancaster such that the Pathfinders could lay down a smokescreen – I assume with the purpose of hiding us from flak, or in some other way to confound the Hun. We flew over to Wyton to give it a try. No-one, however, had thought to check what happens to the airflow through a Lancaster. It creates an area of low pressure around the rear turret, so what happened when we turned the smoke machine on was that it came out of the smoke nozzle jutting through the bomb doors, under the rear fuselage to the low pressure area on either side of the rear turret and then immediately back into the aircraft through the rear, along the fuselage and into the cockpit.

Within moments we couldn't see a thing as smoke was everywhere. It was panic stations all round as we put on oxygen and opened the windows. Slowly, very slowly, the smoke cleared and we were able to land. Suffice to say the experiment never really took off!

The majority if not all Bomber Command squadrons throughout the war featured their fair share of dominion aircrew, men from the commonwealth who had signed up to the notion of protecting their monarch: Australians (immediately distinguishable with their deep blue uniforms), New Zealanders, Canadians (who always seemed to have better cloth), South Africans, Rhodesians especially. Many Americans too, frustrated by the impotence of their government in the early years, crossed over the border into Canada and found themselves part of Bomber Command via the Royal Canadian Air Force. One such 'Yank in the RAF' was Flying Officer Oswald Interiano DFC who had the good grace on one occasion to give me a lift down to Manston so that I might visit my mother. Another was Flight Lieutenant Walt Reif.

Walt was quite a small man but very powerfully built. He was particularly unusual because he was an American of German extraction flying in the RCAF. His dislike for the Germans was matched only for his dislike of the Americans, because at the start of the war his parents – who had moved to the US before the First World War – had been interned as illegal aliens. Reif felt the slight to such an extent that when the US Air Force finally caught up with him and asked him to swap uniforms, he flatly refused.

Reif was a survivor. On an operation to Cologne in October his Lancaster was riddled with flak, but despite extensive damage he managed to bring his crippled bomber home. It was a feat of heroics that might have been recognised with an award, but none was forthcoming. Reif had to settle for the eternal gratitude of his crew who, it is fair to say, worshipped the ground he walked. They were a very tight crew, and looked upon with amused respect by many other aircrew. I got to fly with him just the once, as bomb aimer for an attack on the Heimbach dam but we had to abort because of the weather, a most frustrating experience. It still counted as an op.

Tragedy was to strike the squadron before Christmas. Command was still obsessed with experimenting with its Heavy Oboe idea and organised an attack on the railway marshalling yards at Cologne-Gremberg, a through-route for troops and armour to the Ardennes. This was at the height of the famous 'Battle of the Bulge', and it was vital that German reinforcements were prevented from getting through to take on the hard-pressed US forces holding out at Malmedy and Bastogne. The weather in the UK was foul, and our squadron was briefed on no fewer than three occasions before it was finally allowed to go, taking off in thick fog.

As with our previous sorties with Flight Lieutenant Grant, a 'specialist' pilot from 109 Squadron had been seconded to our unit: this was Squadron Leader Bob Palmer DFC. Playing 'taxi driver' was our own Squadron Leader Owen Milne. Weather conditions were meant to be poor over the target, hence the need for Oboe. They weren't. It was bright sunshine. Orders to bomb independently should Oboe fail were confused. Oboe failed. Chaos ensued. Some of the pilots in the three formations stuck resolutely to their leader and were shot down for their pains. German flak had a field day, as did a flight of German fighters that just happened upon the attacking force, totally by chance. It was, by any definition, a slaughter, with no fewer than eight out of a total of 28 aircraft shot down. Among the dead and missing was Walter Reif. Only his two gunners survived, to spend the rest of the war in captivity. Bob Palmer too was killed, and awarded a posthumous Victoria Cross.

Christmas at Little Staughton was not surprisingly a sad affair, but crews were quickly replaced, and new names began to appear on the Battle Order.

*   *   *

The New Year dawned. 1945. The war in Europe had but five months to run.

Death was part of life in a wartime bomber station, and there were many new faces at breakfast. Among these arrivals was a new squadron commander, Wing Commander Stafford Coulson. Coulson was the epitome of an RAF 'type' with a magnificent moustache that made him an instant pin-up. Coulson had had a frustrating war: originally trained as a fighter pilot, circumstance and illness meant that he had missed most if not all of the major battles until the spring of 1944 when he finally saw action as a Pathfinder. As a flight commander with 35 Squadron he soon gained a reputation for being one of the most outstanding pilots of the unit, and a consummate professional, his achievements being recognised with the DFC and command of 582 Squadron to replace Peter Cribb, who had himself been promoted to command the station.

Stafford's arrival also signalled the start of some high jinx on the station, the like of which had never been seen before. We shared Little Staughton, as I have said, with 109 Squadron which flew Mosquitoes. Stafford's arrival coincided with that of a new CO for 109 in the shape of Wing Commander Robert Law DSO, DFC. Bob Law and Stafford took an instant dislike to one another, and Stafford fed off the undercurrent of superiority that the Mosquito pilots seemed to laud over their Lancaster counterparts.

The Mosquito pilots were brave, there was no doubting that. The problem was that they were not only faster, but they also had a more powerful radio, and so could communicate their desire to land whilst still many miles adrift of our own aircraft, and be ahead of us by the time permission to pancake was given. This meant we had to spend more time stooging around the Bedfordshire countryside, often after a long six or seven hour slog, and wait until our little friends had landed.

Not surprisingly, it bred a little resentment, and so a series of rather petty and ultimately dangerous tit for tat 'raids' were planned and executed, all with Stafford's blessing. The ringmaster was our gunnery leader, who positively excelled in creating a series of pranks that had poor Bob Law fuming. One of the most dangerous by far was the dropping of a flare down the chimney of the 109 Squadron CO's office, that by all accounts caused quite a bit of damage. On another occasion, one of our navigators was caught red handed, just about to set fire to a pile of papers on his desk, and got a swift kick up the backside for his troubles. The incidents came to be known as 'The Staughton Wars' and though I never took part in them myself, it was a perfectly understandable way of letting off steam.

I flew only the once in January, five hours with GOD to

Hanover and back. I was also informed that my promotion to flight lieutenant (again war substantive) had been confirmed. Flight Lieutenant Jimmy Brown DFC was my pilot for another five hour excursion to Wiesbaden on February 2, Bomber Command's one and only large raid on the town involving nearly 500 aircraft. To give some idea of the might of the command at this stage, that same day Harris was able to order more than 300 aircraft to attack Wanne Eickel, and a further 250 bombers to hit Karlsruhe. The total effort for that night was 1,250 sorties.

In cricketing parlance, my operational record was now in the nervous nineties. Whilst I had been operating over the winter, Peter Cribb had clearly been busy. At Staughton my flight engineer leader's hut was directly opposite Peter's office where he sat with the adjutant and the orderly. One morning I was sitting in my office not doing a great deal when the orderly came running across and burst into my room, effusing his congratulations. I didn't know what he was talking about so he told me that I had been awarded an immediate Distinguished Service Order. I told him not to be so stupid, and that flight engineers don't get DSOs. He said, "That's as maybe Sir but look!" At that point he thrust the signal into my hand and sure enough it was true. It was from Harris and it read: 'Warmest Congratulations on the Award of your DSO'. As usual it was the orderly sergeant who knew everything before the rest of us! The award was official as from February 16, 1945.

Of course I was delighted, and most intrigued when I finally got to read the citation for the award that referred to a raid back in October when, according to Martin Middlebrook, I bombed the wrong target. The words written by Peter Cribb (a shortened version ran in the *London Gazette*) read as follows:

> "On October 12, Flight Lieutenant Stocker volun-
> teered to be bomb aimer and flight engineer to the
> master bomber for a daylight attack on the oil works
> at Wanne Eickel in the heart of the Ruhr. The attack
> was opened by a well placed TI aimed by Stocker and
> the master bomber continued to circle the area for 10
> minutes during which time the aircraft was under

almost continuous fire from many heavy guns and was hit in several places. A further bombing run was directed by Flight Lieutenant Stocker with equally satisfactory results and throughout he assisted the master greatly by his accurate commentary on the bombing and by his indifference to the opposition.

Flight Lieutenant Stocker's conduct on this occasion was exemplary and in accordance with the high standard of courage which he has shown on a great many occasions in his long operational career."

In the original recommendation forwarded by Cribb to Bennett, 'Fatty' Collings had added his own comments:

"This officer showed courage, skill and devotion to duty of the highest order in efficiently carrying out the hazardous task for which he volunteered. This, combined with his exceptional operational record, makes him very worthy of the Immediate Award of the Distinguished Service Order."

Most interesting of all, looking back over these documents more than 60 years later, Peter Cribb submitted his recommendation on December 24 1944, where he had already credited me with 100 sorties. Collings added his remarks on December 29, and Bennett a few days later. It was to be four months later, however, that I would actually reach 100 sorties. By February 16, I was still six short.

Exactly a week later on the morning of February 23, Group asked for a master bomber and various supporters for an attack on Pforzheim. We chose eight names to put on the Battle Order, with the pilot selected to lead the raid being a South African, Ted Swales.

Swales had worked his way up through the Pathfinder ranks and was incredibly keen to learn more from anyone who could teach him. He had been awarded an immediate DFC after the Christmas Cologne/Gremberg raid where he had fought off continuous fighter attacks and still made it home. He had an easy approach to him, and was always good company in the mess. He was also rather modest. Of course he did rather stick out in his khaki battle dress, but I don't believe any of us at the time knew that pathfinding was his second wartime 'career', and that he had actually spent the early part of the war as a soldier fighting in the western desert. I think that only came out after he was killed, when the full extent of his bravery in action was revealed.

Sadly the raid on Pforzheim was Swales' last. The attack was a complete success, but Swales' aircraft was hit by a nightfighter over the target. He headed for home, and managed to keep the aircraft aloft long enough for all of his crew to escape by parachute and survive. Unfortunately for Swales, he was too low to abandon the aircraft himself and attempted a crash landing. He struck some power cables and the aircraft exploded. It was a tragic end to a gallant airmen who had died so that others might live. Like Palmer two months before, Swales was awarded a posthumous Victoria Cross, one of only three awarded to Pathfinders in the entire war.

Whilst February was a quiet month for me in terms of operations, I more than made up for it in March when I flew on no fewer than five separate occasions with three different pilots. We hit Cologne on March 2 with Flight Lieutenant Paddy Finlay DFC & Bar at the controls; Hemmingstedt on the 7th (again with Finlay); Dortmund on March 12 with a New Zealander pilot Martyn Nairn; and two trips to Dülmen and Paderborn on March 22 and 27 respectively with another Kiwi, Flight Lieutenant Richard Berney. Berney had been operating since 1941 and had received the DFM as a sergeant pilot with 115 Squadron. (Coincidentally both Nairn and Berney would later receive the Air Force Cross, gazetted in the same issue of the *London Gazette*, September 4, 1945).

The attack on Cologne was my third visit to the city, and the last of the war. American forces captured what was left four days later. The raid on the Deutsche Erdoel refinery in Hemmingstedt proved a disappointment, the bombs missing the target by a good two or three miles. Dortmund had the unhappy record of registering our largest attack ever organised for a single target, with 1,108 Lancasters, Halifaxes and Mosquitoes dropping 4,851 tons of bombs through thick cloud. By comparison the raid on Dülmen involved only 130 aircraft on a relatively quiet afternoon for Bomber Command. All of these attacks, with the exception of our visit to Hemmingstedt, were in daylight, as was the most spectacular, on March 27, when our CO Stafford Coulson, destroyed the town of Paderborn in less than 15 minutes and without losing a single aircraft.

It was by now obvious to us all that the war couldn't last much longer. Raids were being mounted in full daylight with fighter escorts, and the loss rates were so low that they were now counted in single aircraft, rather than percentages. Resistance was virtually nil, although the occasional flak burst might remind you never to relax and we still suffered casualties. There was also still the inevitable risk of accidents and misfortune. Johnnie Gould, a popular 23-year-old flying officer, was lost when his aircraft blew up on the way back from Chemnitz, the result of a faulty illuminator flare; Flying Officer William Underwood DFC and his crew disappeared without trace, whether through accident or enemy action is not known; and Flying Officer Robert Terpening, an Australian with the DFC, was killed when his Lancaster crashed during a training exercise.

I teamed again with Jimmy Brown on April 4 when I clocked up my 99th sortie and my first ever on the oil refinery at Lutzkendorf. The weather was unusually bad that day, and icing proved a problem, as did the flak and the searchlights. Six aircraft were lost and the raid was only partially successful.

Then came the day, at last, for my 100th operation, flying as a spare bod with an Australian Flying Officer 'Hal' Mettam. Mettam was on his 13th trip, and relatively inexperienced, and probably a little nervous of having someone like me onboard rather than his usual bomb aimer. I hoped that 13 wouldn't prove unlucky for either of us!

The target chosen was Kiel, where the Deutsche Werke U-boat yards were still considered a threat, and three capital ships – the *Admiral Scheer*, the *Admiral Hipper* and the *Emden* – were hiding out. It was pretty much a full squadron show. We took off a little after 20:00hrs as part of an attacking force of 591 Lancasters and eight Mosquitoes, with Squadron Leader

Vivian Owen-Jones DFC, one of our flight commanders, in the role as master bomber. The Met Flight (i.e. weather) Mosquito somehow missed the rendezvous or couldn't be heard, and so Owen-Jones ordered a visual attack and we saw the first red TIs going down. We dropped our own green TIs slightly to the port of the line of reds, and a good concentration of bombs began to rain down on the target. We added a 4,000lb 'cookie' and four 1,000lbs bombs to the conflagration below before heading for home, and had the satisfaction later of learning that the raid had been a total success. The *Admiral Scheer* had been hit and capsized, and the two other ships had also been badly damaged. They would not be threatening our convoys again.

After my 100th trip the authorities were keen to keep me on the ground, but since we were rapidly running out of targets to bomb, that wasn't difficult to achieve. There was one target, however, that we all wanted to have a crack at, and the opportunity presented itself, unofficially at least, at the end of the month in a raid that has now gone down in legend in Pathfinder circles, both because of the target and because of the spirit in which the raid took place.

My log book says it all. In green ink, the words 'Base' and 'Base' are written, with a space in-between. In the gap, in pencil so that it could be rubbed out later if necessary, is the target: Berchtesgaden. Hitler's redoubt.

Berchtesgaden was Hitler's equivalent of Chequers, a country retreat where he would entertain his most ardent supporters. He first rented and then bought a small property there after obliging the owner of the principal property to sell it to him and then promptly driving out all of the local residents. Many of his followers also took up residence in the surrounding area, and a magnificent retreat was built known as *Kehlsteinhaus*, or 'Eagle's Nest'. This retreat was more than 3,300ft high, but the mountain itself extended for a further half a mile. Martin Bormann decided that his master deserved an even more commanding view of the mountains — and organised it as a present for Hitler's 50th birthday. A road was blasted into the side of the mountain, but even high explosive could not enable the road to reach the summit. A lift was built into the core of the mountain itself to travel the remaining 400ft to the top; Hitler, it was said, never trusted the lift as it presented too good an opportunity for a would-be assassin.

If you were to ask any Bomber Command veteran which raid he would have most liked to have been on, there is a good chance the answer would have been the raid to bomb Hitler's house. April 25 was to be the date.

As usual I was in the operations room on the morning of April 24 to find out if there was any news of plans for the squadron. The teleprinter from Group announced there would be a raid in daylight the next day but there were no details of which squadrons would be used. The codename for the target was not one that the intelligence officer immediately recognised, so he went and looked it up (all major targets had code words named after fish, for example Chubb was Mannheim, Kipper was Kiel, Whitebait was Berlin etc.). It wasn't surprising that he had not come across it before because he returned to tell me it was Hitler's house at Berchtesgaden.

I guessed that Peter Cribb, even though he was now the station commander, would be interested, (it might be in my best interest too, as if Peter went I would have a better chance of being chosen to go myself). The station commander's office was just across the road from the operations room. I popped across to tell Peter, returning straight away to await Group's signal defining which squadrons would be required for the attack. Within an hour the answer came: 582 was stood down, another PFF squadron was to provide the master bomber and all other markers. Wing Commander James Fordham of 635 Squadron had been chosen to lead the raid with a RNZAF Flight Lieutenant George Hitchcock DFC as his deputy.

I went back across the road to break the news to Peter and waited while he made a 'phone call. From what was said I gathered he was talking to the armament officer about a stock check in the bomb dump where they had discovered four 2,000lb bombs not on the inventory (probably brought back from a raid but not correctly booked back in). The station commander concluded the 'phone call by saying something about 'getting rid of them for you'. He then turned to me to ask if I could round up a crew to visit Hitler's home; I gave him an affirmative answer.

Station commanders do not have their own aircraft, of course, so I had to see the squadron commander, Stafford Coulson, to tell him that the squadron was stood down and that the station commander would like to borrow a Lancaster the next day. Naturally Stafford wanted to know more. I gave him the gist of the proposal, after which he volunteered to be flight engineer. I said that seat was already filled, and so we compromised: I would be bomb aimer, Stafford the second pilot. I went round the squadron offices and very soon had a volunteer crew.

We were all agreed that this was one operation that we were not going to miss. We grilled the intelligence officer about it, and whether he knew any of the relevant codewords. Stafford phoned Group where he had various 'contacts', and although no-one would tell him the route, he did at least manage to discover the H-Hour – so we knew what time we had to be there.

Not knowing the route, we had to make one up, and promptly roped in the help of our squadron navigation leader Dudley Archer (Squadron Leader Dudley Archer DSO, DFC). Dudley was well up for it, as was our squadron signals leader, and our gunnery leader, Squadron Leader George McQueen DFC. We thus had our crew: Peter was the pilot; Stafford was the second pilot; I was the bomb aimer; Dudley our navigator; the signals leader was our wireless op; and McQueen was in the rear turret. This was probably the most experienced crew ever to take to the sky, and I should imagine the combined tally rate of sorties between the five of us was probably upward of 350 trips! We decided to go without a second navigator or mid-upper gunner.

As the take-off had to be very early in the morning, I arranged for the service police to give us an early call. Unfortunately some kind soul subsequently told the police that there were no operations 'on', so we would not need an early call after all. I don't remember who woke up first and called the rest of us. By the time we reached our aircraft 'Z' Zebra (PB969), a relatively new Lancaster III, it was already bombed up with the four 2,000lb medium capacity bombs and the groundcrew were waiting and wondering why we were late.

Dudley said that the only way we could possibly catch up was to take a direct route across France and into Germany. We took off at 06:10 hrs. It was a beautiful spring day. Visibility was excellent as we took a short cut across the French countryside and started to climb to prepare for the attack. The Mosquitoes had arrived on time and climbed to 39,000ft in an attempt to mark the target. Unfortunately, somebody in the planning team had forgotten that there was a large mountain in between the Oboe-equipped aircraft, and the caravan transmitting the signal to bomb. The master bomber, therefore, had to resort to visual bombing, and Hitchcock went in and dropped his TIs accordingly. There was no doubt that everyone who followed wanted to make sure that their bombs counted, and the accuracy of the main force was of a standard not often seen. The SS barracks were largely destroyed, and there were direct hits scored on both wings of the chalet and the private residence of the SS chief.

When we were still 50 miles out from the target we met the stream. It was a magnificent sight, and great to have company flying over Germany in broad daylight. We could see the mountain ahead of us covered in smoke and the majority of the main force had already turned for home. We had a clear run over the mountain and could quite clearly see the aiming point. We had the great satisfaction of seeing our four bombs dropping away and hitting the target. Peter kept the aircraft straight and level for long enough to ensure an aiming point photograph (i.e. a photograph to confirm our bombs were on target) that officially doesn't exist. (After the war, Dudley Archer was part of an RAF team evaluating the accuracy of the command's bombing, and apparently he had great fun trying to account for the destruction caused by our bombs that in theory had never been dropped!)

With a tremendous feeling of satisfaction we too opened up the taps and headed back for base, anxious that we should get back before our ruse was discovered. Unfortunately the cat was already well and truly out of the bag. Whilst we were out, Bennett had 'phoned and asked to speak to Stafford. When he sensed the answers were somewhat evasive as to Coulson's whereabouts, Bennett apparently exploded. Officially, Bennett was informed, the CO, station commander, and most of the squadron's senior officers were all out on a 10-hour cross-country exercise. Bennett's response was not recorded.

To all intents and purposes, the war was effectively over, but operations were still 'on'. The Germans had placed an embargo on all food transports to the western Netherlands after the national railways complied with the exiled Dutch government's appeal for a railway strike to further the Allied liberation efforts. The Nazi embargo was partially lifted in early November 1944, allowing restricted food transports over water, but by then the unusually early and harsh winter had already set in. The canals froze over and became impassable for barges. Food stocks in the cities in the western Netherlands rapidly ran out.

The winter of 1944/45 came to be known in Holland as the Hongerwinter ('Hunger Winter'), and a series of extraordinary factors combined to make their predicament more precarious than usual. The Netherlands was one of the main western battlefields, which wreaked havoc with transport. The retreating German armies had made matters worse by destroying lochs and bridges to flood the country, which in turn ruined what few crops had still survived. In an effort to relieve the Dutch famine, negotiations took place with the German occupiers for coordinated dropping of food by the Royal Air Force over what was still German-occupied Dutch territory. Instead of targets, aircrew were briefed on drop zones. The Germans had agreed on corridors of safe passage and where the drop zones could be located, and so Operation Manna began.

The first sortie on 29 April 1945 (that scheduled for 28 April had to be postponed due to bad weather) involved 242 Lancasters to drop the food and 8 Mosquitoes to mark the drop zones. I flew my only Manna operation on May 1, with Squadron Leader Kenneth Swann DFC in the pilot's seat. To ensure accuracy of the drop and that the food parcels hit the ground undamaged, we flew at very low altitude (typically 500ft or less) and at very slow speed. It was easy to see the huge crowds that gathered below us, all waving and cheering.

It was a magnificent sight. On the ground, green flares were fired to indicate the supplies were landing within the agreed drop zones, and red flares if they were straying into danger zones. A large white cross on the ground marked the centre of the drop zone. (A total of 3,100 flights were made by Bomber Command, and an additional 2,200 by the American Air Force. More than 11,000 tons of food were dropped in the 10 days of the operation.)

Coinciding with our Manna flights were our 'Exodus' trips, returning prisoners of war to England, sometimes after nearly six years of captivity. Flight Lieutenant Anthony Harte-Lovelace was my pilot for May 8 as we flew over to Juvincourt to pick up our first batch of 25 prisoners of war and return them to Wing in Buckinghamshire which had been set up as a POW receiving centre. Harte-Lovelace was on his 50th and what was to prove his final operation of the war. He was an ex-578 pilot prior to joining Pathfinders and came to us with the DFC.[9]

I remember the POWs well. They were a rag tag mob of khaki in some very non-regulation attire, much of it no doubt accumulated over years of incarceration, and their few meagre belonging slung in knapsacks over their shoulders. They were all pathetically grateful and impatient to get home. Some had never even seen a Lancaster before close up, let alone flown in one. Even so they formed an orderly queue as they waited their turn to board, and their discipline was impeccable.

Even Exodus trips were not without their dangers. Disaster befell one 514 Squadron Lancaster that took off from Juvincourt with 24 POWs and was soon experiencing difficulties in control. The pilot, Flight Lieutenant Donald Beaton DSO, tried to make it back to the airfield but crashed killing all onboard. Beaton had won his DSO for an action over Le Havre in September 1944 when his aircraft was hit by flak. He had been seriously wounded by flying shrapnel, and

---

[9]There is a further story to add about Harte-Lovelace. Returning from one of these Exodus trips he elected to fly low over Canterbury to give one of the returning POWs his first glimpse of home after so long in captivity. Unfortunately he was reported for low flying, court martialled, and reduced in rank. He left the RAF in 1948 to become a civil pilot with Airwork and then British United Airways. He died in 1965.

his leg was broken. Despite his injuries, and intense pain, the young skipper refused to leave the controls and landed safely at an emergency field on the south coast. The citation for his DSO described his actions as 'most inspiring'.

Fortunately, our luck held. We had the privilege of flying back over England on the evening of VE Day when bonfires were lit all over the country. It was a magnificent sight. I didn't actually get a drink because we didn't land until the morning of the 9th which was probably sometime after midnight. We then returned to Lübeck airport later that morning, the first to arrive and the last to leave. I took my service motorbike with me and I put that in the back of the Lanc. I used it at the other end to help marshal the aircraft around the field, like a mobile air traffic control officer. The airfield was a fascinating place, only recently abandoned by the Germans so I was more than a little curious. At it happened, I came upon a building that contained some interesting maps. Fortunately, on reaching out for one of the maps I noticed that, balanced at the other end of the map, was a butterfly bomb left as a booby trap. How ironic it would have been to have survived more than 100 raids without a scratch, only to get myself blown up and killed on the first day of peace! I was lucky.

The war was over. I had survived.

*   *   *

By the war's end, I had flown 105 operations (including Manna and Exodus trips), and survived. I flew my first operation, to Essen, on October 11 1941 and my last trip to bomb an enemy target on April 25, 1945.

My flying amounted to 375 hours and 15 minutes by day, and 494 hours and 45 minutes at night, the large majority on operations. It was an impressive record by any measure.

I served with four squadrons throughout the war, with my operations (excluding those that did not count) broken down as follows:

35 Squadron	36 operations
102 Squadron	11 operations
7 Squadron	8 operations

582 Squadron   50 operations

I have always described my time at 582 Squadron as a 'holiday' compared to some of my earlier experiences – although that may seem strange given that I flew nearly as many sorties with 582 as I had with my three previous squadrons!

Between 1942 and 1945, Bomber Command flew more than 300,000 operational sorties. During that period they lost around 8,000 aircraft and a further 1,500 or so were written off as damaged beyond repair. But it is the human cost that is most telling. In six years of conflict, almost 56,000 men – or about half of the 125,000 aircrew who served in the command were killed, 8,400 injured and a further 11,000 were missing or held as prisoners of war. Out of any 100 airmen who joined an operational training unit (OTU), half would be killed on active operations, a quarter would be killed on combat operations or in non-operational accidents, and a dozen or so would become prisoners of war. Only a handful of the original 100 would make it through unharmed.

Different experts at the time and since have tried to analyse our chances of survival, which seemed to vary considerably depending on what years were being compared, and how many operations had been flown. There was a secret memorandum circulated in the Air Ministry in 1942 that suggested that aircrew on heavy bombers had only a 44 percent chance of surviving their first tour. The percentage of those expected to finish a second tour (assuming they survived their six-month 'rest'), fell to 19.5 percent. By early 1943, the chances of survival fell further still. By then, only about 17 percent of men could be expected to finish 30 operations in one piece, and a mere 2.5 percent would survive two tours. I survived four; I assume the likelihood of me or anyone else surviving more than 100 heavy bomber operations would not feature on a percentage chart, but there were a few of us that made it, to confound the mathematicians. Wing Commanders 'Tubby' Baker and 'Willie' Tait, for example, both exceeded 100 heavy bomber sorties. As did Wing Commander Edward 'Dipper' Deacon DSO DFC who was a contemporary of mine at 35 Squadron and whose record stretched back to 1940. But we were the exception that disproved the rule. Of those who made it to the century mark, men such as Alec Cranswick who possibly holds the record for heavy bomber sorties (Bennett credits him with 143), nearly all of them were killed. Then there were the tragic cases of those gallant airmen shot down on their 97th, 98th or 99th sorties, men such as Danny Everett, Victor 'Davy' Davies DFM (of 582 Squadron) and others.

The odds against survival were simply too great.

I have always believed that operations became less risky as the war progressed, primarily because less time was spent over enemy territory. From start to finish, I have looked at the average duration of each sortie:

Year	Average operational flying time (per sortie)
1941	Six hours
1942	Five hours and 50 minutes
1943	Six hours and 15 minutes
1944	Four hours and 25 minutes
1945	Five hours and 45 minutes

On the face of it, the least risky period in which to fly a tour of operations with Bomber Command – given the assertion that less time in the air meant less chance of being shot down – appears to be 1944, but this is worthy of further investigation.

From January to April 1944, my average sortie lasted seven hours and 30 minutes – actually longer than any period previously. This average was brought down significantly in May, June and July 1944 when Harris was obliged to divert his forces to support the army immediately before and after the invasion in Europe. I actually flew both my longest and my shortest trips during the war in a period of less than 10 days: a nine hour and 20 minute operation to Stettin on August 29, 1944 followed on September 6, 1944 with a daylight to Le Havre in which I was out and back in precisely two hours!

The first few months of 1944 in fact proved to be the most lethal for a good many Pathfinder crews. On the night of January 1/2, for example, 156 Squadron lost four entire crews over Berlin; all 28 men killed. One of the captains, Squadron Leader Rowland Fawcett DFC, was on his third tour of operations and had flown not less than 69 trips. Two other members of his crew were decorated. Another captain, Squadron Leader Ronald Stewart, a married man of 23, had similarly flown not less than 49 ops, and four other members of his crew held either the DFC or DFM. The next night, the same squadron lost a further five aircraft and their crews, from which there were only four survivors. The maths is simple and alarming: nine aircraft shot down and 59 men dead in less than 24 hours. One of the dead, Sergeant Ronald Hillman was only 17 years of age.

Other Pathfinders suffered similarly appalling casualties that night and afterwards: 83 Squadron lost four aircraft, with not a single survivor left to record their story. And on the night of January 5/6, 35 Squadron lost two aircraft, including one piloted by 27-year-old Flight Lieutenant Robert Appleby DFC with whom I had flown earlier in the war. He was last heard by another aircraft transmitting his position over W/T and maintaining height on three engines. Only one of his crew made it out alive.

January was indeed a disastrous month for Pathfinder force. Another of my former units, 7 Squadron, lost three crews on the 14th attacking Braunschweig (Brunswick). Among the dead was Flight Lieutenant David Thomas who had flown not less than 44 sorties. As if they hadn't suffered enough already, 156 lost a further five aircraft with a further 30 men killed. One of the skippers was Wing Commander Nelson Mansfield DFC, a 31-year-old regular officer with some 53 operations under his belt. Within his crew were Squadron Leader Edward Alexander DFC, DFM, who was also a second tour man at least, as well as two other decorated aircrew. Before January was out, another senior officer, Wing Commander R. E. Young DSO, DFC from 7 Squadron had also been lost, shot down over Berlin. He survived. Even with the war virtually won, good men were still being lost and continued to be killed right up until the final days.

I took part in virtually every major battle of the European air war, including the battles of The Ruhr and Berlin, and bombed almost every major target, some of them frequently. Essen, for example, I visited on no fewer than seven occasions between October 11, 1941 and April 26, 1944, and other 'favourites' included Lorient (six times) and Bremen (six times). I 'only' went to Berlin on four occasions, when many crews were lucky to survive the experience once.

I have never felt the need to post-rationalise the bombing war or my part in it. After the fall of France and the Battle of Britain, Bomber Command was the only viable weapon with which we could prosecute the war, and take the fight to the Germans. I bombed cities, heavy industries, port installations, oil refineries, transport networks, military barracks, rocket sites, gun emplacements, dykes, and even the holiday retreat of the Führer himself. My log book stands as a fascinating historical record encapsulating Bomber Command operations, almost first to last, and certainly from start to finish of the subsequently controversial tenure of our ultimate 'boss', Arthur Harris.

By the end of the war the force that we could muster on a daily basis would have seemed unbelievable to the early pioneers venturing out with their leaflets in their Whitleys and Hampdens. In 1945, Harris had a daily average availability of 1,420 aircraft, 1,305 of them being four-engined heavies. To the end of April, Bomber Command flew 67,483 sorties and dropped over 181,000 tons of bombs – one fifth of the total of the entire war; 608 aircraft failed to return – or less than one percent of the attacking force.

Perhaps by the end of the war I had become blasé about my chances of survival. Perhaps, unknowingly, I had become a little 'flak happy'. Who is to say? What can be said, however, is that I was a survivor. I stayed alive when others were dropping dead all around me. I went through more than 100 raids and the worst damage I suffered was a few holes in my jacket. Why did I survive? Luck – although experience no doubt helped that luck along. I never took unnecessary risks. I didn't drink too much if it looked like we might be operating, but if we were stood down I could drink with the best of them. I didn't smoke in the aircraft, and I would discourage others from lighting up. Smoking affected concentration, and night vision, and there was always the risk that the light from a match or a cigarette lighter might be seen by a marauding nightfighter. It was better not to take the chance.

I flew a good many trips as a spare bod; some crews I was happier to fly with than others. If I ever thought a crew was dangerous, I avoided them, and avoided flying with them again. By the end of the war, with my operational record, some were a little in awe of me, and that was perhaps to my advantage. It kept them on their toes.

The quality of crews generally improved as the years went on. In the early days, when I first started operating, there were still those pilots, nearly all of them regular officers, who saw the rest of us as a nuisance. They believed we had volunteered simply because it was a fast way to earn promotion, and because there was extra pay involved. We joked that we were paid ballast. But later this impression changed. Pilots began to realise that survival depended upon operating as a crew. There was particular acknowledgement, for example, of the importance of a navigator. A pilot could be a skilful flyer, but if he couldn't find his way to the target, he was all but impotent. Respect became the watchword, respect for one another's duties and responsibilities. This was particularly so in Pathfinders, where the ability to interchange roles was essential. I read that it cost an average of £10,000 (at 1940s prices) to train each member of a bomber crew, enough to send 10 men to Oxford or Cambridge for three years. Arguably it was an investment well spent.

I was indeed the lucky one. But remember this: for every one that was lucky there were hundreds and in some cases thousands that didn't make it.

CHAPTER SIX

TOURING

The war in Europe may have ended, but the war in the Far East still had nearly four months left to run, and the RAF began preparing 'Tiger Force' to support the final push and the ultimate invasion of Japan. Any hopes of me joining such a force, however, were dashed in the middle of July when I was asked to join a 'special duties' flight. Of course we didn't know what we were letting ourselves in for beyond that it wouldn't be what we had been used to. Over the next few days we had various vaccinations and drew a quantity of special kit, including some tropical gear, and were given a couple of days to pick up civvies.

Squadron Leader Bob Cairns was to be our pilot, and at the CO's conference on July 18 we were told that we had been chosen to escort Air Chief Marshal Sir Arthur Harris on a good-will tour of Brazil. With that, we collected a new Lancaster, one of the new Lancaster VIIs – coded NX689 – with Merlin 24 engines, and flew an air test very early in the morning of July 19 to get used to the aircraft and the rest of the crew. Later that same day, Cairns flew an Oxford (an Airspeed Oxford twin-engined training aircraft used as the station 'hack') down to Staverton, with me onboard, for a more detailed briefing of what was required.

The flight, it transpired, would comprise three aircraft, all crewed by highly experienced officers not just from Pathfinders, but representative of the whole of Bomber Command:

NX687 'A' Abel   Wing Commander C.C. Calder DSO DFC
and crew

NX688 'B' Baker   Wing Commander A.J.L. Craig DSO DFC
                    and crew
NX689 'C' Charlie   Squadron Leader R.M.B. Cairns DFC and
                    crew

'Jock' Calder had latterly been a 5 Group man having volunteered to fly with 617 Squadron in late 1944. He was a true Bomber Command veteran, however, having started his tour of operations on Whitleys with 78 Squadron before becoming a flight commander with 76 Squadron flying the Halifax. Awarded the DFC by the end of 1941, he was appointed officer commanding 158 Squadron and later chief flying instructor at Marston Moor Heavy Conversion Unit before joining the legendary 'Dambusters'. With 617 I believe he was credited with dropping the very first of their 12,000lb Tallboys.

Allan Craig was also a veteran who was the last wartime commanding officer of 156 Squadron. A Volunteer Reserve sergeant pilot, he had been commissioned in July 1941 and won his first DFC whilst with 7 Squadron in July 1944, the citation crediting him with 'a large number of sorties... demanding a high degree of skill and resolution'. He added the Distinguished Service Order a few months later in the rank of acting squadron leader, and completed more than a dozen trips as master bomber.

Bob Cairns was a Scot, who was also inevitably christened 'Jock' by his crew. He too had an impressive wartime career. An officer of the Volunteer Reserve, he was trained at 83 OTU and 1667 HCU before joining main force as a pilot with 625 Squadron. Keen to move onto Pathfinders, Cairns joined 582 Squadron after less than a dozen trips, and flew from Little Staughton until the war's end, by which time he had completed around 50 operations (including the deadly Cologne/Gremberg raid), at least one as master bomber, and been awarded the DFC.

My fellow crew members included two navigators – Flying Officer Roddy Rodwell and Flight Lieutenant Fred Croney, a wireless op – Flying Officer Bill Hough, and Flight Lieutenant Cooper as gunner. With the exception of Cooper, the rest of the crew were all 582 Squadron veterans.

The aircraft were resplendent in their white paintwork and black undersides. All radar equipment except Gee had been removed, as had the bomb and gun sights. The rear turret was fitted with 0.5 inch guns and the mid-upper turret had been removed in order to make provision for a passenger. For the passenger, a Rumbold-type chair was installed with the necessary fittings, intercom, oxygen and some instruments and even a window. The undercarriage was re-inforced, and a 15-gallon water tank was fitted within the fuselage and various spares carried in the bomb bay.

On July 21 we flew an endurance test. This was important as we had some long sea crossings ahead of us. We went from our temporary base (Wyton) to Gravesend, Dungeness, Lille, Dijon, Marseilles, Bordeaux, a point in the Bay of Biscay, Land's End, Douglas (Isle of Man), Flamborough Head, and back to Wyton, in all a flight of nine hours, 55 minutes. The next morning we found out that we would be crossing the South Atlantic from West Africa to Recife in northern Brazil, a distance of around 2,000 miles, so we were pleased we had tested the endurance of the aircraft to the full.

After a sleepless night, the crews awoke excited and tired. The morning was spent loading the aircraft and immediately there was a problem. The amount of spares being carried meant the crews' luggage had to fit in the fuselage, which meant space was at a premium. This minor inconvenience overcome, we took off at 15:10 to St Mawgan in Cornwall, our start point. It was the first time all three crews had rendezvoused and met, and briefing was scheduled for 10:00 the following morning.

The briefing confirmed the route: the flight to Brazil would take place in three stages: St Mawgan to Rabat (in French Morocco); Rabat to Bathurst in the Gambia; and finally Bathurst to Recife – a total of nearly 24-hours flying. It was then a further six hours from Recife to Rio. Every aircraft was to carry VIPs. The honour of transporting the air chief marshal, his PA (Flight Lieutenant Peter Tomlinson) and a batman fell to Wing Commander Calder. Wing Commander Craig would carry Flight Lieutenant Prettiman and his four-year-old daughter, the former being attached to the UK's embassy in Rio. I would fly with the Brazilian air attaché in London, Colonel Hocksher. We would also carry four groundcrew.

Take-off went without a hitch at 23:12. The evening flight would take us over the water to the west of Spain and Portugal. Even at 6,000ft it became noticeably warmer and thick cloud meant that we had to drop our height down to 700ft. We had no trouble in finding the airfield near Rabat (Salé) and let down after exactly seven hours in the air. It wasn't a very attractive place and there were flies everywhere. Being a civilian airfield, we were obliged to clear customs before we could get breakfast, but nobody seemed very hungry.

During breakfast we heard that Harris' aircraft had developed a fault (oil had found its way into the port inner coolant tank), and the next leg was postponed for a day for repairs. Any thoughts we had of disappearing off into Rabat for the night, however, were dashed when it was decided that the air chief marshal would swap to 'B' Baker and carry on as scheduled. Craig would have to stay until a new engine arrived and follow on later. Our passenger, Colonel Hocksher, would also stay behind, and Prettiman and his daughter would come with us.

'C' Charlie was in the air again the next morning at 11:20, and cruised down the west coast of Africa at around 6,000ft. There was not much for any of us to do except admire the clear blue sea and sandy beaches. The wireless op, Bill Hough, would contact 'B' Baker by R/T every hour to report, and for a brief period we flew in formation – the only time during the entire trip that any two aircraft had visual contact. After about four hours flying we ran into tropical storms. We could see the weather but had no choice but to go through it. Although wet, it was not as bumpy as a thunderstorm might be in the UK, and we made landfall at Dakar, 100 miles from our destination. With some difficulty, including the loss of all radio communication with the ground, we at last found Bathurst and then Yumdum airfield, which looked for all the world like an emergency strip carved into the jungle.

Bob kept losing sight of the runway, and it was only on our

third approach that he finally managed to get us down. We bounced three times before we finally came to a halt, rather too close to the end of the runway for our liking. When we got out we could see that the runway was only packed clay with a metal mesh on top, and with all of the rain it had become incredibly slippery. In the circumstances, Bob did very well, and it was easy to see why they had decided we needed a reinforced undercarriage.

The accommodation for the evening was more comfortable than initial impressions might have suggested. An eight-mile drive through jungle brought us to a BOAC 'camp' where a large number of friendly locals descended upon us to carry our luggage and take us to our rooms. Having bathed and changed, dinner was in the company of Harris and various top brass from BOAC.

Bill, our wireless op, suggested to Harris that we had the next day off as we were all very tired and he agreed. It was a good idea as it gave 'A' Able a chance of catching us up again. Dinner the next evening included tropical fruits the like of which we hadn't seen in years, if at all, and plenty of champagne. There was a rather rowdy party in the BOAC mess and then off to bed. Overnight we were surprised to hear that Churchill had been kicked out, and labour had won a landslide election.

For the last leg prior to reaching Brazil, the journey would be almost entirely over sea, and although the Met forecast was good, three destroyers (two American and one Brazilian) were strung out along the route to act in an air-sea rescue role should disaster strike. Furthermore they were each equipped with beacons that would be switched on for five minutes in every hour to help with navigation. 'A' Able, however, had still not arrived and so the decision was taken to push on without them.

Soon after take-off, Bill had trouble with the radio and so changed the modulator in the transmitter and that seemed to fix it. We weren't able to contact the first destroyer so pressed on. We were able to contact the second destroyer, and the crew of 'B' Baker and exchange positions. They were five minutes ahead of us. Soon after mid-ocean where we changed control from Bathurst to Natal, both Bill's transmitter and receiver packed up, and he was left with only R/T for communication. There wasn't much he could do except sit back and admire the scenery, such as it was, as we were over sea!

The Lancaster droned on, crossing the equator without any of the crew realising it. We failed to make contact with the third destroyer but eventually made landfall a little north of our estimated track and had to fly down the coast to Recife. 'B' Baker was already on the ground as we arrived overhead, and landed without incident. The taxiway was lined with Brazilian troops and units of various Brazilian forces were waiting on the tarmac as we parked. Harris and the other passengers were wearing North American khaki tropical uniforms with long trousers but we, the aircrew, had been issued with normal overseas khaki uniforms with shorts, not acceptable in that region of Brazil. We were told to get back in the aircraft. Harris inspected the troops and took the salute. Then we were whisked away, with sirens blaring, to a hotel on the sea front where we soon had our heads down.

That evening there was a seven course banquet waiting for us. We poor aircrew had to put on our normal UK blue uniforms and sweat it out. There were plenty of high ranking Brazilian officers in attendance in uniforms that made ours look drab by comparison. The food took some getting used to, especially after six years of rationing. We had steaks so large that they filled your plate, and actually you couldn't eat it all, not with our shrunken stomachs. After dinner it was off to the British expatriate's club and it seemed that our visit was big news – so big that the local school children had been given the day off to see us.

The last leg of the journey beckoned. Being awoken the following morning at 05:00, we were on the airfield for 06:30 prior to a scheduled take-off at 09:00. 'A' Abel had just landed, and her crew had dashed off for a meal and a wash. With the welcoming ceremonies at Rio arranged for 15:00, the other two aircraft again had to forge ahead in the hope that Abel would catch up in time. Flying down the coast at c6,000ft, we made our landfall and reduced height to 2,000ft for a flypast of the city and the bay: it was a beautiful sight seeing the enormous bay being effectively 'guarded' by two massive rocks. It really was a wonder to see.

We caught sight of the airfield and had to take a double look. It was situated on a peninsular of land jutting out from the bay, only one runway with water at each end and on one side and a little over 3,000ft in length. It would take quite a bit of skill to land here, we thought, so we made a steep approach and came in without any problems. In front of us, 'B' Baker had already landed, and immediately behind us – having made up time – was 'A' Abel so we were once again reunited. (As I understand it, the Americans were most impressed but also a little bit miffed by our landing. Apparently they had said it wasn't possible because they hadn't been able to land their Flying Fortresses there).

The Lancasters landed at Rio, and would stay there for the next 10 days. The airfield was named after an early Brazilian aviation pioneer, Alberto Santos Dumont, and once again there was a large welcoming committee of the great and the good as well as thousands of civilians to greet us. Various representatives from the Forca Aerea Brasiliera (FAB) – the Brazilian Air Force – took the junior and senior officers off to their billets, in my case the Copacabana Palace Hotel. There then followed five days of receptions, parties and clubbing, and not all of them 'official'. The Brazilian hosts were at pains to provide their British friends with the finest hospitality, and we were treated like royalty wherever we went. The local community really took us under their wing.

On July 31, the tour party was taken to an aeronautical college and on August 2, I was flown down to São Paulo, 150 miles south of Rio, in a Lockheed Loadstar to spend two days in the city. São Paolo was in the heart of Brazil's coffee growing region, and Brazil's largest industrial town. We were treated to a demonstration of 'skip' bombing by a formation of six FAB Boston aircraft, but the display was marred by news that one of the aircraft had crashed killing all onboard. Even in peacetime, with nobody firing at you, flying was still a dangerous occupation.

The pace of official duties for Harris soon took its toll, and on August 3 he was forced to spend a day of rest while Wing

Commander Calder deputised in his stead. The rich food had apparently proved that it was possible to have too much of a good thing. The next day I was flown in a DC3 from Cambica back to Santos Dumont, and promptly bundled into a car to drive up into the mountains for yet another open air lunch and on to Petropolis for an overnight stay in the Hotel Quitandinha, reputed to be one of the most luxurious in the southern hemisphere.

I remember clearly a flypast given by one of the aircraft during our stay, and the amusing outcome: coffee in wartime Britain was of course in short supply, but the Brazilians had it in abundance. They gave us various sack-loads of the stuff that they tied into the bomb bay of the 617 Squadron aircraft ('Jock' Calder's 'A' Abel). The trouble was that the 617 Squadron Lancaster didn't have any bomb doors and we had great pleasure in watching them take off and bombard the local harbour with coffee beans!

The official programme ended on August 6 – the day the US dropped the first of their two atomic bombs on Japan – giving the party three free days before the scheduled departure on August 10, but only after we had met and shaken hands with the president of the United States of Brazil (as it was known then). That evening, Harris and the three Lancaster captains, Calder, Craig and Cairns were presented with one of Brazil's most important decorations, the National Order of the Croix du Sul (Southern Cross). Harris was appointed to the Grand Cross, and Calder, Craig and Cairns were appointed 'officers'. Calder, it is interesting to note, already had his fair share of foreign 'gongs', having earlier in the war been singled out by the Russians for one of their Medals of Valour.

The evening before we were due to say goodbye to Brazil, Bob Cairns told us that we would be receiving an early call, but a little later announced that we wouldn't be going after all, because 'A' Abel required yet another engine change and my experience was required. Out of the three flight engineers, I was the only one with a true engineering background, and so it was clear that I had to stay and help. This met with a mixed reception from my colleagues, some of whom were anxious to get back but there were worse places we could think of to be stranded. When the replacement engine finally arrived, instead of being a Merlin 24 it was a Merlin 22 with different fittings. It meant that we had to wait even longer for the correct engine to be delivered. Our crew were no longer guests of the Brazilian government; the local ex-pats rallied round and Roddy Rodwell and I stayed with an Englishman, a bachelor with five staff including a cook, a steward and a maid. He ran a card school once a week, and a couple of his friends were big-wigs in tobacco and telecoms. Their idea of money was very different to mine.

In the event, parts – and a team of fitters – were sent to convert the 22 to be able to fit within the 24 mounting, and all was well. I was at dinner the night of August 14 when news came through that the Japanese had surrendered, and the Second World War was at last at an end. It was the cause for much celebration.

With the new engine at last fitted, and our allegiances – and luggage – transferred to a new aircraft ('A' Abel), we set off for the short 30-minute trip from Santos Dumont to Santa Cruz, before a longer six-hour flight to Natal. It had been an early start but I think we were all very glad to be on our way, if only to escape the heat. We arrived at Natal, an FAB base, just after 18:00, and were up early again the following morning to fly to Georgetown, in what is now Guyana. Flying over the Amazon basin was particularly memorable, especially the contrast of the muddy river with the bright blue sea. We had to battle through a tropical storm, which meant it got rather bumpy, but we were able to find the airfield (Atkinson Field) easily enough and land without any difficulty.

Atkinson was a US base carved out of the jungle. Being US, food was aplenty and we visitors were treated royally by our hosts. The heat, however, was causing problems for us all, and sleep was increasingly difficult. The next leg of our journey would take us to the Caribbean islands of the Bahamas, and all of us paid particular attention to the Met forecast, given that we were in the middle of hurricane season! It was another brief stop-over, and we were put up at the Royal Victoria hotel. It looked most impressive from the outside, but as it turned out, looks can be deceptive. None of us thought much of the town either, and it was raining so all in all it was a million miles away from the Caribbean depicted in the glossy holiday brochures of today.

By now, the sense of adventure that we had enjoyed earlier was beginning to evaporate, and thoughts were turning to home. We were displeased, therefore, having left Nassau and arrived in Montreal, to be told by the chief technical officer that our aircraft was due for a major inspection and that it would take 72 hours! Despite the protestations of the skipper, Cairns was forced to back down in the knowledge that the CTO had the power to ground us indefinitely if we didn't comply. As it was we struck a compromise, and by the afternoon of the following day (August 26) an air test was possible and the aircraft cleared for the next stage of our journey, from Montreal to Goose Bay.

We followed the St Lawrence for a time and then flew over Quebec City before heading for the isolated airfield at Goose Bay. Nobody was keen to stay too long, and it was decided to fly the next leg overnight. We were rewarded for this with a spectacular view of the Northern Lights, but afterwards there was little to see other than the Atlantic. Our route took us to the southern tip of Greenland, although we couldn't see it, and then on to Reykjavik – a most inhospitable looking place with its lunar landscape.

Everyone was tired, having missed a night's sleep, and at the briefing the next day the briefing officers expected us to finish our transit in Prestwick which none of us wanted to do. We couldn't see why we couldn't go directly to St Mawgan which was well within range. The forecast wasn't too good but we decided to press on regardless. As it happened, we were not able to reach St Mawgan or Prestwick; the weather closed in to such an extent that St Mawgan was shut down, and the wireless operator received a message to say that we could try the Fleet Air Arm base of Merryfield if we wished. In the darkness, and with a low cloud base, the airfield was difficult to find but find it we did and landed at 20:43, closely followed by a Liberator that had similarly been diverted from St Mawgan and had been stooging around for the past half hour looking for a break in the weather.

The customs officers were very quickly onboard but as you can imagine we weren't too keen on showing them what we had brought back with us. Cairns told them that most of our luggage was in the bomb bay along with a load of aircraft spares which would take hours to unload and reload, and that perhaps it was better left undisturbed. Fortunately the officer seemed to swallow this tale, and so we were left to our own devices. This was probably the most frustrating time for all of us. Although we were back in England, we were still miles away from home and our home base, Wyton, was also closed. We learned that Mildenhall was open, and being close enough, decided to try for there.

In all the trip had lasted seven weeks – considerably longer than we first expected. Flying time totalled 77.25 hours, during which time our modified Lancasters performed admirably, notwithstanding the earlier need to change engines. I was pleased to be home, and ready to embark on yet another adventure in what was proving to be an eventful career.

* * *

With the war over and the first of my 'special' duties completed, I began thinking seriously about my future. Having joined as an aircraft apprentice, my immediate thoughts were to continue within the air force. It was, after all, my chosen career, unlike many of the thousands I had flown with that were simply in 'for the duration'.

In the meantime, however, it was decided that I would be sent on an engineering officers course at 4 School of Technical Training. Nearly all of us on the course were flight engineers, mostly Bomber Command (although there were some fitters from Fighter Command), and quite a few us were ex-apprentices.

It was generally understood that a flight engineer in wartime had been trained to do a specific job for the specific difficulties we faced at that time, but that an engineer in peacetime would need to know a whole lot more besides. The course was mostly theoretical, rather than practical, although I do recall being asked to weld aluminium for the first time. Mostly we were looking at the theory of the internal combustion engine, fuel efficiencies etc. – it was much more scientific than wartime training had allowed. Although jet aircraft were now in service, jet bombers were still a little way off, but I should imagine that the Air Ministry had half an eye on where things were heading and our course was tailored accordingly. Later, of course, flight engineers would be replaced by the 'crew chief' system, and after the event it was easy to understand why we were being schooled in such a way.

My desire to 'stay in' as an officer came about on September 1, 1945 when I was granted a permanent commission 'as a flying officer in the general duties engineering branch of the Royal Air Force'. All of us had been asked but not all of us had got it. Mine was a permanent commission that effectively meant a full time career and I was delighted. Some of the others received an alternative that meant they were covered for flying duties but there was a ceiling on their promotion and an age at which they were obliged to retire.

My course ended in April 1946 after which I received orders to report to 1359 Flight as part of Transport Command at RAF Bassingbourn on the Hertfordshire/Cambridgeshire border. Bassingbourn had been a well-known US Air Force base during the war, and the airfield from which the famous 'Memphis Belle' flew her final mission that meant everlasting fame for her skipper and crew. By the time I arrived it had been handed back to the RAF, and the station commander was Group Captain (later Air Marshal) Ronnie Lees – a quite marvellous character who I liked instantly. Ronnie was an Australian who had joined the RAAF in 1930 and fought both at Dunkirk and in the Battle of Britain, winning the DFC in 1940 and a Bar the following year. By the end of the war he had been on the staff at HQ Mediterranean Allied Tactical Air Force, having at one time led no fewer than five Spitfire squadrons in North Africa and Italy.

This was where I got my first look at a Lancastrian, taking a flight with a Squadron Leader Adams in Lancastrian 727 on June 17, 1946. The Lancastrian was simply the 'civil' version of the Lancaster, and looked virtually identical albeit that the gun turrets had been removed and the nose lengthened. In all other respects its dimensions were the same as that of its military sibling. It could carry nine passengers by day, but was only allowed to carry six VIPs at night. Every three seats would convert to a single bunk and above these three bunks was a matching bunk stowed high up against the fuselage wall to be let down at night. The Lancastrian's fuselage was less than half the width of the York's, so the passengers sat facing sideways. A gangway on the starboard side led down to a galley, and reached through a narrow door up a step onto the top of the bomb bay.

Our Flight was soon consumed within 24 Squadron, commanded from September 1946 by a New Zealander Wing Commander C.W.K.Nicholls. The squadron had originally been formed in September 1915 and later became the first DH2 fighter squadron to reach the Western Front. In the Second World War it had been part of Ferry Command, as Transport Command had been known, delivering first mail and later VIPs in Dakotas over long range. It had only moved to Bassingbourn from Hendon in February, a few months before my arrival, and had on its roster a selection of aircraft including Dakotas, Yorks and Lancastrians.

The unit was a commonwealth squadron and so packed with Australians and New Zealanders and there was rarely a dull moment. One of the pilots was no-less than Joe Petrie-Andrews, a former 35 Squadron colleague who had achieved notoriety in his Pathfinder days as being a bit of a daredevil and non-conformist, often finding himself on the wrong side of the authorities. There was no doubting his skills as a pilot, however, as I found out for myself on a number of local trips.

Our squadron's raison d'etre at this point was as a glorified taxi service for the great and the good. We achieved some fame for the work we did running 'the Moscow shuttle' of which little has been written, but provides one amusing story I recall well. With the 'shuttle', our crews would fly our VIPs as far as Berlin, and at Berlin, our wireless operator and navigator would be replaced by a Russian wireless operator and navigator in order to continue the flight on to Moscow. We then reversed the scenario on the return flight.

One day, I was duty officer when one of our Lancastrians returned and I went out to meet it. Imagine my surprise when the back door opens, and I'm confronted by a Russian soldier pointing a tommy gun at me! It transpired that as well as Very Important Persons, we also carried Very Important Cargoes – the cargo in question this time being millions of pounds worth of gold bullion. As I understood it, the bullion was destined for the Russian Embassy in the US, via the UK, but this gave me a bit of a problem. I couldn't leave the gold or the soldier on the aircraft overnight, so I had to find a safe place to store them both. One of the Russian aircrew who had accompanied our own pilot spoke a little English and told me that the soldier and the gold were not to be parted. The solution presented itself when I shared our little problem with the station armourer. He suggested that the obvious place was the armoury set aside for small arms, and so we duly moved all of the gold – and our soldier with his tommy gun still pointed at anyone who went near him – into the armoury overnight. I wasn't on duty the next day and so still don't actually know what happened to the gold, but I believe the Russians sent a fleet of cars to take it away. I assume they let the guard out of the armoury too.

All of our VIPs were treated to the very highest standards of service that the military could offer. We had a number of air quartermasters (AQMs) who were responsible for the passengers once they were onboard, whilst we just did the flying. No expense was spared on the crockery, for example, which was the finest Wedgewood and locked away in a secure store overnight. If any of the plates were broken, it is the only time I ever saw a special order form being required to get it replaced. No expense was also spared on either the food or the drink. There would be tinned fruit, fresh fruit, cakes, and more mundane but equally essential items such as tinned meat, beans, spaghetti, bread, cheese, eggs, salads and soft drinks – although these were primarily for show. One of our passengers, an extremely well known member of parliament at that time, was capable of drinking a bottle of scotch on the short trip to Paris, and finish another on his return leg (or should that be legless!).

A particular incident that does stay in the mind, because it could so nearly have ended in disaster, resulted from a series of flights in October taking a number of senior officers – among them the former 5 Group commander Sir Ralph Cochrane and the inventor of radar, Sir Robert Watson Watt, over to the PIACO conference in Indianapolis.

I was flying in Lancastrian VM735 with my then regular pilot, Flight Lieutenant Milne, one of two flight engineers onboard. Having flown from Northolt to Largens, our first stop over, we needed to refuel before taking on the nearly 10-hour haul to Bermuda. While we waited for the petrol bowsers we fitted an extension to the belly tank filler. When the two refuelling tankers arrived, I went to the port wing and the other flight engineer the starboard, to fill the wing tanks. While we were doing this, a third, smaller tanker appeared and the driver started to fill the belly tank. Once I had finished what I was doing, I jumped down to see why the driver seemed to be having trouble getting the fuel into the tank. He was continually stopping and starting.

Not speaking his language, I motioned to allow me to take over. On removing the nozzle to check the fitting of the tank filler, you can imagine my horror when I saw that we were being refuelled with engine oil. With the AOC-in-C onboard we decided drastic action was called for and managed to get the rear of the aircraft off the hard standing and over the grass. Here we disconnected the outlet from the belly tank transfer pump, then added some petrol to the oil in the tank and dumped the mixture of petrol/oil onto the grass. We did this several times until the flow was reasonably clear. I then removed the fuel transfer pump, stripped it down, washed the parts in a bucket of petrol, reassembled and refitted the pump and then refilled as normal and moved the aircraft away from the contaminated ground.

In the end we weren't delayed and I'm not even sure if the senior officers onboard knew what we were doing. It meant we missed out on our ground meal before taking off, so that was a little annoying. It does make you wonder though, whether this sort of thing had happened before. Our old flight commander in 582 Squadron days, Brian McMillan, was the pilot of the 'Star Tiger' that went missing over the Bermuda Triangle with 'Mary' Coningham (Air Vice-Marshal Arthur

Coningham) onboard, and nobody knows to this day what happened to him. Could it have been as simple as the wrong type of fuel?

In all we spent the better part of two weeks flying around the States, delivering our 'brass hats' to their required destinations, including another well known name, Air Marshal Sir Victor Goddard who had been a senior staff officer at the time of the retreat from Dunkirk. From Bermuda we flew to Washington, and then from there to Indianapolis where the conference was being held. Other destinations in my log book include Langley Field, Nassau, Miami, Greenville and New York, before heading up to Montreal and then home to Lyneham via Gander – in total some 60 hours of flying. It was more than a little tiring and we were pleased to be home.

(Whilst on one of our stopovers, we did see one particular sight that would later play a significant role in my service career. Parked at the airfield in Indianapolis, was one of Lockheed's latest designs that had just landed after a record-breaking flight from Perth, Western Australia to Columbus, Ohio. The aircraft was named Truculent Turtle – a Lockheed Neptune – and I was later to become supremely well acquainted with its successors.)

One of the things after the war that became a regular bind was the need felt by the Air Ministry constantly to assess the capability of its aircrew. As such, I was forever being tested, both formally and informally, as regards my suitability for handling certain scenarios or duties. This would then cause you to be awarded certain 'categories' – for example cleared to carry cargo – or the highest level of categorisation when you were cleared to carry VIPs. My report from the Transport Command aircrew examination unit is a case in point, the detail noting:

"No 50954 Flight Lieutenant Stocker EE: the above-mentioned flight engineer was examined by this unit in accordance with TCASI Vol IX No 4 Appendix 'D', and was awarded the following category: 46/T/Lancastrian/'A' cat."

It was dated November 20, 1946 and signed by the examiner, Flight Lieutenant William Earnshaw. It meant at least somebody was happy with me and I had a certificate to prove it.

For a large part of my time at 24 Squadron I was unfortunately sick and unable to fly. It was primarily a recurrence of the problem that had troubled me since Halton. For eight years I had suffered from frequent headaches above my left eye, and these were becoming more severe. In the January of 1947 I was banned from flying for a period and seen regularly by doctors every second week. Passed as fit in March I flew with Flight Lieutenant Le Hardy in a Dakota down to Honington and back, not realising that this would be the only flying I would do for over a year. In April I was hospitalised as my sinuses were blocked, and I had contracted conjunctivitis as a result of being poked in the eye accidentally by my small son. I was examined by the Medical Board in May, whilst still in hospital in Ely, following a further operation to cure what was diagnosed as being osteoma of the frontal sinus. They seemed much happier with me and sent me on 14 days leave. Unfortunately I then went down with tonsillitis and a temperature just short of 103.

It was a miserable time, as no sooner had I recovered from one ailment, than I went down with another. The only thing that cheered me up, however, was when I received an invitation from the Chancery of the order of knighthood to attend Buckingham Palace, again, to be invested with my DSO. The date was December 9, 1947, nearly three years after the deed that had won me the award. I remembered from my previous visit to the palace not to shake the King's hand too vigorously, and to be careful when taking my bow. I also remember being caught short a little before the ceremony itself, and being led by an attendant to a washroom that was quite simply one of the most beautiful and luxurious I have ever seen. The toilet seat was in mahogany and it seemed a pity to sit on it.

Christmas passed, and a further Medical Board was held in January 1948 after which I was officially declared as being fit for duty, although it was several months before I was once again in the air. It was a gentle reintroduction to flying, with a series of local flights with Flight Lieutenant Mellor to Bassingbourn and Brize Norton, and similar sorties undertaken with a number of different pilots and different aircraft (Lancastrians and Yorks) to get me back into the fray.

On June 29, 1948 I was obliged to take a most bizarre expedition to Accra, via Castel Benito. We had been briefed to take a psychiatrist from RAF Northolt to our base in Accra to replace the resident psychiatrist who – ironically enough – appeared to have gone mad. Certainly his behaviour was giving the locals cause for concern, and so we carried two male nurses with us in order to bring him home. The flight itself over the Sahara was most pleasant, although long, requiring a refuelling stop along the way. This I remember well as the weather conditions had adversely affected the fuel supplies which were saturated with water. There was nothing we could do except filter the fuel, by hand, through a chamois leather and into the tanks. Needless to say it was an arduous, laborious task that took hours, but we felt a little safer that the water wouldn't cause the engines to stop mid-flight.

When we arrived at Accra, the two nurses made sure our 'patient' was comfortable. One of them had been resident nurse to Rudolf Hess, the deputy führer, during his captivity after he had flown to Britain in a warped scheme to sue for peace and seemed to be very much in control. During the return trip from Accra to Castel Benito, a flight of more than 11 hours, I needed the toilet, and so set off to the back of the aircraft where the loo was located. As I passed the patient, who was unrestrained at this point (because of the turbulent conditions he was sat on the toilet) I noticed on the fuselage wall an emergency axe in a case, with the words above it saying 'in an emergency chop here'. Nobody else seemed to be particularly concerned, or perhaps they hadn't noticed it, so as subtly as I could I removed the axe from its case, and slid it into my jockeys. Now this axe had a particularly sharp blade at one end, and a needle sharp point at the other, so I walked as gingerly as I could back to the cockpit, praying that we wouldn't hit any bad turbulence along the way! Fortunately we didn't, and I was able to remove the axe from my trousers without any damage being done.

By now, the world had changed. Trouble was brewing in Malaya and I found myself once again on a war footing. Until 1945, the British had been arming communist guerrillas in Malaya to fight the Japanese. After the Japanese had been kicked out, the Malayans then started using these weapons, and the presence of one million Chinese in Malaya, to attempt to seize power. A state of emergency had been declared in June, and the British, under the command of Lieutenant General Sir Harold Biggs, began offensive operations to cut the rebels from the principal sources of supply. Progress was hampered in the early days of the conflict by a lack of adequate airfields or landing strips, which meant replenishing supplies of guns and ammunition to our forces was a problem. Our squadron, given the capacity and endurance of our Lancastrians (our aircraft had a range of c4,150 miles at 200mph), were therefore called in to help.

On July 16 we set off in Lancastrian VL980 skippered by the A Flight commander Flight Lieutenant Flowers with a load of small arms and ammunition from Bassingbourn to El Adem. The next day we were off again early (our take-off time is noted as being 05:45) for the next stage of our journey but as we powered over Abyssinia (Ethiopia) I noticed one of the engines was overheating and was obliged to shut her down. With such a long way still to run, and over hostile territory, we decided to put down in Aden (Khormaksar). After quite a bit of toing and froing and a number of telephone calls it was finally decided that an Avro York would fly out with a replacement Merlin 24 engine, and we would transfer our cargo onto the York to take out to our troops. I would be left, in the meantime, to supervise the engine change. I wasn't best impressed as I was due to go on leave in a couple of days, and in the event had to spend a week in Aden with just one corporal to help me make the switch. We worked solidly between us in a metal hangar where, as you can imagine, the heat at certain times of the day was quite literally unbearable. Still we managed to sweat it out and get the job done, and on July 24, Flowers took the Lancastrian – replete with new engine – for a 50 minute air test before declaring himself satisfied. By the late afternoon of the 26th, we were at last home where some good news awaited me.

My time at 24 Squadron was at an end. And a whole new chapter in my career, and my life, was about to begin.

CHAPTER SEVEN

PILOTING

The timing came out of the blue. While I had always wanted to be a pilot, and the thought of piloting my own aircraft had often excited me, when the order did come through to report to 7 Flying Training School (7FTS) at RAF Cottesmore I was a little taken aback.

The course was comprised almost exclusively of other aircrew: there was one squadron leader air gunner (this was George McQueen who had been the gunnery leader at 582 Squadron and awarded both the DFC and the US DFC), and the rest were flight lieutenant engineers, navigators and wireless ops. I know that we all outranked our instructors! Although we didn't know it at the time, our little group of trainee pilots achieved some historic significance by being the last course ever to learn how to fly on the Tiger Moth. We knew in the end, because one of our tasks was to fly the aircraft back to their maintenance unit (in Kemble) where I think they were to be broken up or sold off. 'My' aircraft was T7129. I recall standing by flying control, not yet having been awarded my wings (that followed later in the course) but with my flight engineer's brevet and squadron badge showing and somebody saying: "Blimey, they even let flight engineers fly these things now!"

But I am a little ahead of myself. The Tiger Moth, officially designated the DH82a, was arguably the most respected training aircraft certainly of its generation, and possibly of all time. It was a development of the highly successful Gypsy Moth which preceded it, from the redoubtable aircraft manufacturer De Havilland. It was quite tricky to fly and had very sensitive flying controls – certainly in comparison to the

Prentices and Chipmunks which followed and which were positively benign.

My first flight was with a pilot instructor P IV Cooke (they started at this time to use strange ranks for our NCO pilots), a familiarisation flight of 25 minutes. That was July 30, 1948. In the first week of August I flew on the 4th, 5th, and 6th, my training following a similar pattern the following week. By the end of August, on August 31 to be precise, I was let loose in T7040 for my first solo, having completed about 16 hours dual. I don't remember much about it but my log book shows that I flew once in the morning with P II Durys (a most understanding man!) and then he must have jumped out and let me have it. I flew twice more that day, including another solo.

Instruction, of course, was not only in the air. We also had to satisfy our instructors that we had sufficient knowledge of the fuel, oil and ignition systems of the Tiger Moth, as well as how to start the aircraft, swing the propeller, and what to do in the event of an emergency. I flew throughout September and October – climbing, descending, stalling, medium turns, climbing turns, tight turns, spinning, taking off and landing – all manner of disciplines to show I was safe in charge of one of His Majesty's aircraft before a test with what I imagine was the chief flying instructor Squadron Leader Petch and then finally taking to the air with the OC C Flight, Flight Lieutenant Clarke, for my final handling test.

I must have made a good enough job of it because in December my training progressed to the much faster North American-built Harvard. The transition between the Tiger Moth and the Harvard was quite significant. The Tiger Moth was an open-cockpit biplane powered by a 130hp Gypsy engine (which I had worked on at Halton) capable of a maximum speed of around 109mph; the Harvard, on the other hand, was a monoplane with an enclosed cockpit, and with a huge Pratt and Whitney 550hp Wasp engine capable of powering the aircraft to speeds in excess of 200mph. It also had retractable undercarriage, which was another feature to remember, especially when landing.

Flying training on the Harvard began on December 4 (my

first flight was in Harvard FX338) and my first solo (in FT412) followed on December 20. Meantime I had taken yet another test to certify my knowledge of the Harvard's inner workings, but it wasn't until the following July that I was finally awarded my wings, and only after I had displayed sufficient prowess not just in flying, but also navigation, steep glide bombing, and gunnery. My final handling test was given to me by Wing Commander Davis who wrote on August 10, 1949 that I was 'average' as a single-engined pilot, 'average' as a pilot navigator, 'average' at bombing (clearly I had lost the knack since my days on Pathfinders) and 'average' in air gunnery.

I believe I am right in saying that every one of our course got through. Perhaps the Air Ministry had decided, given our rank and experience, that it would be embarrassing to them if we were to fail. What I do know is that all of our instructors were unusually understanding and patient with us, and certainly worked very hard to ensure we succeeded. Next came the postings, and I was delighted that I was going to heavies. McQueen was similarly delighted that he was going to fighters/ ground attack, and later lost his life, I was told, flying a De Havilland Hornet, the successor to the Mosquito.

After a few weeks leave, and with my new pilot's wings sewn over my left breast pocket, I set off for 201 Advanced Flying School (AFS) RAF Swinderby to be re-acquainted with the Vickers Wellington, but this time a more powerful variant than the one I had first seen at Boscombe Down. The Wellington I was to fly was known as the Wellington T10. A T10 was effectively a 'reconditioned' Mk X, which instead of being a bomber, had been transformed under license with Boulton Paul to become a training aircraft complete with faired nose in place of a turret. (So successful was the T10 that it remained in service until 1953 when it was superseded by the Valetta T3.) I had my first dual control (in PF991) with a Flight Lieutenant Thieme on November 10, and took the controls myself on November 21 with some gentle circuits and landings, a theme that was to continue for the next few days. By December 16 the course was completed, and I was once more presented with an assessment of my flying skills that once again confirmed me as 'average'.

After my first Wellington solo I was given my first crew: a navigator/second pilot for the solo flights and cross-country exercises, and on some exercises a wireless operator. The wireless operators were on the staff, so we never had the same one, but the navigator was ours for the duration. My navigator was Flying Officer Thomson and I remember him well. His parents belonged to a strict non-conformist religious sect, and not only did they not approve of him being in the armed forces but they also disapproved of the demon alcohol. The son did not share his parents' disapproval.

It's fair to say that the RAF was in no particular rush to see me trained. I left Swinderby early in the new year of 1950, and reported to operational conversion unit (OCU) at Kinloss on February 15 where I was at last to be re-united with the Lancaster, but this time in the pilot's seat. Flight Lieutenant Simpson had the pleasure of my company for my 'first' flight in a Lancaster – the aircraft in question being RE186 – a Lanc originally intended as an air-sea rescue variant but converted for training purposes. During my stay at OCU I was able to secure myself a 'regular' crew comprising:

PII Guidotti
F/O Samuels
N3 Capern
S2 Cartlidge
S2 Livermore
S1 Webb
E1 Poulter

My time at Kinloss was comparatively short, but memorable for two reasons. The first was my ability to have incurred my commanding officer's displeasure. His name was Wing Commander Holgate, and I believe he had been Coastal Command all through his career. He obviously had something of a chip on his shoulder and it came as no surprise when he ranked me only as 'average' in my flying and navigational expertise and even 'below average' in instrument flying – something I simply wasn't any good at. Instrument flying practice was primarily conducted in what was called a 'Link' trainer – in effect a primitive flight simulator – and Holgate made a point in my assessment of suggesting that my 'general flying lacks polish, particularly the landings'. That is strange, because I don't recall any of my crew ever complaining about my landings. (Later, as an aside, I do remember one landing I made where I held off perfectly, and there was only the faintest of bumps as I brought the aircraft onto the ground. So delighted was I with my performance that I couldn't resist going on intercom and announcing: 'pilot to crew. Just in case you're wondering, we've landed.')

The second memorable incident at Kinloss was an escape and evasion exercise where we all ended up in Elgin Prison. The exercise was quite a major one, involving all three armed forces, army, navy and air force, as well as the local police and volunteer game keepers. As was usual in such circumstances, groups of us were piled into the back of a lorry and driven out to the middle of nowhere and dropped off in pairs. Each pair was supposed to make it to a particular rendezvous point without getting caught. I was with a naval officer who I had met when we were both turfed out of the lorry together and for the first few hours we made good progress. With the night closing in we decided to find shelter and came to a little hut that contained a large quantity of beaters that were used to put out fires. We managed to make a bed out of these and keep ourselves fairly warm. We tucked in to our flying rations – chocolate and barley sugars – and waited until morning. At first light we set off again and headed for the coast. Between us and the coast, however, was a main road, and since we were in fairly open ground, we had no option but to make a dash for it. Unfortunately, just as we made it onto the road, a police car turned up and we were arrested. They took us to Elgin gaol which had been emptied especially for the exercise, and where the 'interrogations' were due to take place.

The exercise was due to finish at 18:00, when all of the genuine prisoners were supposed to be moved back in. By now it was about 17:00, and they wanted to transfer us from the prison into a barbed wire compound outside. I didn't fancy that much, so as we were being marched out, I helped myself to the key to the door that sealed the particular block we were in. Chaos ensued. The prison officers couldn't move the prisoners back in without the key, and I wasn't going to give it up that easily. I therefore waited until 6:00 p.m., and the exercise was officially over, before owning up that I had it. The police were not best impressed, but then neither was I in being kept out in the cold.

(Incidentally, one of the airmen on the exercise was Harry Kerr. He was a Scotsman who had originally been a wireless op but retrained as a pilot on the same course as me. He was 'captured' early on in the exercise, and subjected to some fairly harsh treatment. The interrogators were trying to get us to tell them the co-ordinates for the rendezvous point, but neither Harry nor I obliged, even though Harry was stripped and thrown naked into a coal bunker!)

If my stay at Kinloss was short, my stay at 120 Squadron, RAF Leuchars was shorter still. No sooner had I arrived on June 18, 1950, within five weeks I was posted to a new squadron, 203 at St Eval, but this was not before I was able to cause a little excitement along the way. Leuchars was notoriously prone to fog, and one afternoon I was due to fly down to St Eval (it must have been part of the exchange – several crews had been posted to 203 Squadron at once) and on-board I had a number of senior NCOs and ground staff, all experts in their respective trades. The top of the fog was around 600ft, and as I cleared the runway and began climbing, we were soon in clear air. All was well until the wireless operator reported smoke and the smell of fire near his position. At this point the NCOs all wanted to help, and began taking my aircraft to bits to try and find the fault. It was a tricky situation because there was no way I could get back down to Leuchars, and so had to call Edinburgh for permission to land. It wasn't an emergency, but I was in trouble, and so broadcast a 'Pan Pan Pan' alert (i.e. slightly less critical than a mayday) to let them know I was coming in.

The problem at the time with the airfield at Edinburgh, however, was that the runway was apparently too short for big aircraft like Lancasters. It was around 1,000 yards and we needed something like 1,400 yards. By this stage, however, I didn't have many options left and so came in at very high power, but very low speed, so that when you cut the power the aircraft sinks like a stone. I managed to get it just right, and we pulled up short of the end of the runway with everyone and everything still very much intact. Once on the ground, the groundcrews very quickly located the problem – there had been a minor short in the wireless set – and we were soon on our way again. Coastal Command didn't believe in parachutes, and with all of those men onboard, it was quite an uncomfortable feeling.

Much of my time at 203 was spent in maritime affairs, often flying with a US naval captain seconded to the RAF, Walt Muller, on air-sea rescue (ASR) searches, or practicing the dropping of life rafts into the sea, not surprising since I was now part of Coastal Command. St Eval had achieved fame in the war as one of the primary bases from which the force flew its anti-submarine and anti-shipping sorties to protect the south west coast.

One flight, some time into my stay with the squadron, states simply an ASR to Shannon in the Republic of Ireland. But there is a story behind this. During public holidays, people living in married quarters were allocated the 'standby' duties, and on this particular day (it was Easter) I was the designated captain of the standby search and rescue aircraft when we got a call to try and find an aircraft missing in the mid-Atlantic. Because of the extreme range we were advised to use Shannon to allow more search time in the target area. It took us two and a half hours to get to Shannon where we then refuelled to continue our duties. We were airborne for a further five and a half hours but with no luck.

Clothing, at this time, was still rationed at home and most of the crew, including myself, were smokers. Whilst the aircraft was being re-fuelled I saw the BOAC station manager and persuaded him to cash a cheque for me. With the cash I then went to the custom free shop to buy a length of fine tweed to make a suit for my wife, then to the bonded warehouse to buy a box containing several 200 cigarette cartons for every smoker in the crew. To get them released to the plane, as the captain of the vessel, I had to sign that the cigarettes were for *consumption on the voyage* which I was happy to do, even though I never permitted smoking on a Lancaster.

Returning to St Eval, our aircraft should have been met by the station duty officer who was supposed to act as a customs officer. By the time we landed, I had finished my spell as captain of the standby search and rescue aircraft and was now the station duty officer, so I promptly reported myself as having *nothing to declare*!

*   *   *

At the end of August, 1951, I was summoned to the CO's office and informed that I had been selected for a special operation. I was told that I was to take a group of aircrew and groundcrew to the Lockheed aircraft factory in Burbank, California, where we were to learn to fly a new aircraft that was going to be introduced into Coastal Command and replace our Lancasters. Indeed our mission was not just to learn how to fly the things, but also then to bring them home. The aircraft in question was the latest variant of the exact same aircraft I had seen on my last visit to the States: a P2V-5 Neptune.

It was obviously not without a little excitement that I packed my things and took the train to Paddington and then on to Heathrow (which in those days was a mere fraction of the size it is today) for our flight to the US. We boarded on one of the massive BOAC Boeing Stratocruisers – me and 59 passengers in the safe hands of the pilot, Captain Watson. I had known Watson during the war and he very kindly invited me onto the flightdeck. The journey was in several parts: we first flew from Heathrow to Keflavik, and then from there to Dorval. After an overnight stay, we flew on to Idlewild where we then switched aircraft onto one of the equally impressive TWA Constellations, built by Lockheed who we were shortly to visit. On our way to Los Angeles we were forced to divert to Chicago because of bad weather (our aircraft was actually struck by lightning), finally making it to Los Angeles on September 4.

There was plenty to keep me busy along the way. Whilst in New York, we were obliged to stay over because it was Labour Day and everything was closed down. Some of the boys decided to head into town, whereas I headed for bed. Some time in the early hours of the morning I received a phone call from the city's night judge and told that he had a man with him with no identity, and no money, who had claimed to have been robbed and similarly claimed to have been one of my party. I was happy to confirm that he was indeed one of my men, and then promptly went back to sleep.

The media, as is so often the case, was there ahead of us in LA and we discovered that we were big news. This was because the purchase of the aircraft had been facilitated through MDAP – the Mutual Defence Aid Programme – to help Coastal Command (to whom the aircraft would be going) fulfil the reconnaissance responsibilities required of it by NATO directives. What that effectively amounted to was that we had them 'on loan' and as such they had to be (ultimately) returned. A press release was also issued which ran:

> "...these officers and men of the RAF will study operation of the US Navy's latest P2V-5 anti-submarine patrol planes before flying the new aircraft home for Maritime reconnaissance duty with the RAF. Purchase of P2Vs by Great Britain as well as Australia was published earlier this year concurrently with announcement of this new model by the manufacturer. At that time, the planes were described in Parliament as 'especially valuable for their exceptional endurance.' – Arthur Henderson, speaking as Secretary for Air.
>
> "Proved in service with the US Navy since 1945, the P2V has been America's prime anti-submarine aircraft. It was the first weapon developed specifically to meet the ominous challenge of the snorkel sub. As it has been in the US, the P2V-5 will be exceptionally efficient in patrolling the extensive coastlines of both England and Australia. The new design, however, is not restricted to patrol duty. The airplane carries appreciably more radar and electronic equipment in addition to heavy (*sic*) armament than any previous model. In its primary role as sub-killer, the P2V-5 is prepared to meet the enemy on whatever terms he

may elect. An early Neptune established a record which still stands for long-distance non-stop flight without refuelling, 11,236 miles from Perth, Australia, to Columbus, Ohio. With compound engines, latest model P2Vs extend their range still farther. P2Vs were the first production airplanes to adopt the powerful compound engines, which gain extra propulsion from otherwise wasted exhaust gases.

"These airplanes are in quantity production at the Lockheed aircraft factories, where RAF representatives are studying. After checkout in the P2Vs by Lockheed experts, the RAF will spend some time observing US Navy operation of the aircraft before returning to England."

The photographers were also there to capture a group shot as we looked over the aircraft on our first day of training. The training was comprehensive, and it was to be almost a month spent in the classroom being taught about the aircraft before we were finally allowed to get in and fly one.

The P2V, as the press release articulated, was originally designed as a long-range patrol bomber that was just too late to see war service, having been delivered to the US Navy in December 1945. The Neptune followed in the same mould as its predecessors the Hudson and the Ventura, both of which had been manufactured in considerable numbers during the war for ocean patrol and anti-submarine operations. Unlike earlier Lockheed designs, however, the Neptune was significantly larger, featuring a far greater all-up weight and introducing a tricycle undercarriage. The original production version of the aircraft, Truculent Turtle, had been the aircraft I had seen four years earlier after its record-breaking flight from Australia, piloted by Commander Thomas D Davies. The flight had taken place between September 29 and October 1, 1946, and took 55 hours and 15 minutes. The Neptune had been specially modified for the flight, operating at a loaded weight of 85,000lb, and using a rocket-assisted take-off! Talking to a fairly senior USN officer much later he told me they had trouble reaching their cruise altitude as the rockets were fired too early.

The version that we were to fly was the P2V-5, which was the first of the series to have flexible guns in the nose, as well as featuring enlarged wingtip tanks, a searchlight, radar and the ability to carry extra fuel. (The RAF later modified many of the aircraft to have Plexiglas noses instead of a gun turret.) The Neptune was powered by two 3,250hp Wright Turbo-Cyclone R-3350-30W which would give it a maximum speed of 353mph at 9,500ft with an initial climb of 2,620ft/minute. Service ceiling was 26,000ft, and she had a range (unmodified) of 4,200 miles. To give some idea how this compared, the Shackleton MR3, which had come into being at much the same time, had a range of only 3,660 miles, a top speed of 302mph, and climbed at only 850ft/minute.

My first flight took place in Neptune P2V-5 5028, with one of the Lockheed test pilots, Mr Setili, at the controls. We also had with us one of my fellow pilots from the UK, Flight Lieutenant Dawes from Banstead, Surrey. I continued to fly with Mr Setili and later two of his compatriots Messrs Sulliven and Martin, doing local circuits primarily, and some basic night flying. Joe Towle, chief pilot for the Lockeed Aircraft Corporation certified my log book in October 1951, by which time I had completed 16 hours of dual during the day, and one hour at night, getting to grips with the aircraft.

Our instructor flight engineer was an Englishman, a naturalised American and we hit it off straight away. He was extremely helpful and enabled us to appreciate the technical qualities of the aircraft very quickly. Unfortunately, for this part of the story at least, the log book that covered the next three months was destroyed by the Air Ministry after I had left the RAF – for what reason I have no idea. All I do know is that I spent a thoroughly enjoyable three months in the US, although I never did quite get used to waffles, maple syrup and bacon for breakfast.

I did soon get used to driving on the wrong side of the road, however. Being in the pay of the Americans, as the commanding officer I was obliged weekly to drive into LA to collect our wages. I had been given a car by Lockheed, and headed into town, but had to pass through a busy intersection along the way. Usually this was tricky enough, but on this particular morning the lights at the junction were broken, and police were everywhere, blowing their whistles and waving their arms. It was most confusing, especially at one point when I thought I had been told to advance, when in fact the policeman was indicating something entirely different. At that point he got rather angry and leaning in through the window demanded to see my papers. I reached into my pocket and pulled out my little red British driver's license at which juncture the policeman looked at it and said: "Goddam Limey, I might have known it. Just get the hell outa here!" And so I had my first brush with the American law.

Worse was to follow one afternoon. Driving along the Hollywood freeway was a delight. There was a minimum speed of 50mph and a maximum of 55mph, that gave hassle free motoring. Unfortunately, getting off the freeway was easier said than done, especially when you have the misfortune of the engine overheating and stopping. With my engine not turning but cooling down, other cars simply proceeded to ram into me and push me along before I was finally able to restart the engine and continue. During the time I was at Burbank my UK licence expired, so I took the US driving test instead. The exam was no problem but my examiner said I was too trusting of other drivers as there were a good many drunk drivers around. In its own way that was a sobering thought.

In amongst my driving experiences, I also became proficient on the Neptune. It was particularly light on the controls, especially compared to the Lancaster, and was considerably more manoeuvrable. One of the reasons for this was that it had spoilers on the wings that were controlled by a switch in the cockpit. The spoilers meant there was more drag on the downside wing when you were in a turn. With the spoilers 'on', short strips on the top surface of the wing came up when the aileron was raised. So when you put the stick over, these strips acted as extra ailerons and so made the turn much tighter.

On a Lancaster there were just the two elevators. The Neptune had an additional piece fitted between the elevator and the fixed part of the tail that allowed a variable camber on the tailplane. This meant greater control in the dive; you could make the dive steeper or more shallow simply by adjusting the relevant buttons on the front and rear of the control column. Again, it was simple innovations such as this that made all the difference in the end product.

Of course the Neptune also had considerably more technical equipment onboard including two radars: a search radar and an attack radar, both of which had a level of reliability we had never experienced before. There were also other nice touches. The soundproofing was such that you could talk to your co-pilot without having to use the intercom. It was a wholly different environment from the Lancaster; we had a galley, for example, including its own coffee percolator and even a small oven, which was dead handy if ever your hands got cold!

We ended up staying in the US longer than originally envisaged, but being part of the Lockheed organisation we got to see a number of remarkable aircraft, including the enormous Lockheed Constitution, an aircraft to rival the 'Spruce Goose' of Howard Hughes' fame, but an aircraft that proved similarly ill-fated. The four-engined giant had flown into Burbank from Honolulu and we had a good look around. The 92-ton beast could carry up to 168 passengers and fly from California to Tokyo in 19 hours. One of the most remarkable sights was the addition of a fireman's pole to allow the crew to slide down from the cockpit and escape to the lower decks in the event of a crash landing. It was a remarkable design.

After our training at Lockheed we flew our two new Neptunes with RAF markings to the United States Navy (USN) base at Whitby Island in Washington State. Here we were given more instructions on the military aspects of the aircraft, even being shown how to approach an aircraft carrier in an emergency.

During one training flight, on the approach to land I had a most unusual message from air traffic control: "go round again," the voice told me. "There is a house on the runway." Disbelieving but peering ahead, I could see that they were indeed correct. A typical American wooden house on a multi-wheeled trailer was using the out-of-use runway to get from one side of the airfield to the other. My approach coincided with its slow passage across the runway that was in use, and where I myself needed to land. I managed to get down without further incident.

When our training with the USN finished, we flew the two Neptunes to a United States Air Force (USAF) base over on the Atlantic coast. Here we were to be in the charge of the Military Air Transport Service (MATS). This is where my problems started. MATS had a rule that twin-engined aircraft were not allowed to fly directly across the Atlantic Ocean. The first flight plan they offered was to fly to Bluey West in Greenland, then on to Reykjavik in Iceland before the final leg to Prestwick in Scotland. It was mid-January, and I considered their route to be an unnecessary risk. They seemed to have no idea of what type of aircraft the Neptune was, or what it was designed to do. They clearly did not want to listen, either, so I decided to be as bloody-minded as they were. If they were insisting I fly to Scotland, then I would do it in one go, without stopping. This provoked a more sensible discussion and we eventually agreed a more realistic route to St Eval via the Azores. Thus the first two of 52 Neptunes for the RAF arrived at St Eval on January 27, 1952 to equip 217 Squadron. This was yet another Coastal Command squadron that had disbanded at the end of the Second World War having served assiduously in an anti-submarine role in the Middle and then Far East. I found myself posted to the squadron on the day it was reformed, January 14 1952, and flew in the first of two Neptunes (coded WX493 and 494) for trials.

Back in England there was similar media interest following our return. We were visited by no less a figure than William Sidney, better known as the 6th Baron de L'Isle and Dudley. Sidney had won the Victoria Cross during the defence of the Anzio beachhead and after the war he had entered parliament as conservative MP for Chelsea. In 1951 he had been appointed Secretary of State for Air under the Churchill government, and it was in this capacity that he came to see our new aircraft, with the press never far behind. He seemed genuinely interested in the Neptune, and wanted to know what made it so good. I didn't spare him any blushes, and told him particularly about the reliability of the electronics – something that we hadn't been used to. I didn't think it hurt to tell the truth.

With the media spotlight away from us, we now had the chance of settling down into routine squadron life, and deploying our aircraft accordingly. To this end we were greatly helped by our commanding officer, Mick Ensor, who had a superlative war record in anti-submarine warfare.

Mick Ensor learned to fly in New Zealand and joined 500 Squadron at Bircham Newton, Norfolk in 1941. Having survived several dangerous operations in Blenheims over the North Sea and the French coast, Mick first earned fame on his second Hudson operation in January 1942, attacking three German ships at dangerously low level – so low that his wingtip actually brushed the sea. By superlative flying he managed to limp home, despite having to shut one engine down and losing all of his instruments. During 1942, he hunted U-boats over the Atlantic from Stornoway and then took part in Operation Torch, the Allied invasion of North Africa. Mick destroyed U-259 on 15 November in one of the war's most dramatic attacks. His depth charges exploded prematurely, catching his aircraft in the blast. Two of his crew were killed, but luckily Mick survived, and the U-boat was confirmed as destroyed.

After six months at Coastal Command HQ, sharing his front-line experience with experts conducting the vital Battle of the Atlantic, Mick returned to operations with 224 Squadron in July 1943, flying Liberators. At the age of 23 he had earned no fewer than four decorations for gallantry. After the war, Mick flew 200 missions in the Berlin Airlift and served for two years with the US Navy, where he learned to fly the Neptune. As a result, he was the most experienced pilot on the type, a pilot's pilot, and the ideal candidate for leading the first Neptune squadron.

Mick was a remarkable character in every sense. There was no doubting either his courage, or his flying ability, but there was no doubting either that he missed the war. Whilst he would rarely, if ever, mention his war record, and indeed seemed almost embarrassed by it, he was not a man who cared for peacetime flying, and hated administration. As his senior flight commander, he was happy leaving the administration of the squadron to me, which meant I did most if not all of the donkey work.

One of my tasks was to organise our entry into the Dunning Cup, named after Edward Dunning who had carried out the first successful landing on the deck of a ship, and lost his life attempting the same feat a few days later. The cup was awarded to the squadron that attained the highest standard during the year on the course at the Joint Anti-Submarine School in Londonderry, Northern Ireland. Tactics, signals procedure and air-sea exercises were all judged and scored, and we were particularly watched for the quality of co-operation with our navy colleagues. Competition was keen, and it was a great feather in our cap – and indeed great credit to both Mick and the Neptunes – that we should emerge triumphant. It earned Mick the Air Force Cross.

Further excitement was to follow a few months later (by now it was July 1953) when we took part in the Queen's Review, flying down from Kinloss to St Mawgan (near St Eval) and back in a round trip of more than 1,000 miles. Mick was in the front of the formation of six aircraft, with me effectively in the middle of the box ready to take over if something went wrong. Of course nothing did, but with timing critical, I had one of the most uncomfortable jobs, flying in the dirty air caused by Mick's aircraft for more than five hours. (I had also only recently overcome a touch of gout that had caused some pain in my joints.) We made the rendezvous over RAF Odiham perfectly, part of an impressive flypast that involved 49 separate formations, with each formation 30-seconds apart. More than 630 aircraft (including 18 Shackletons and three Sunderlands) took Her Majesty's salute in less than half an hour. By the time we landed back in Scotland, I was drenched in sweat and totally exhausted.

We had another duty to perform in connection with the coronation celebration, when Her Majesty visited Glasgow. There was to be a review in a large stadium, above which the RAF in Scotland organised a flypast. Our squadron, 217, again flew the vic of five with me flying the sixth aircraft 'in the box'. The difference this time was that instead of my regular co-pilot

I had an ex fighter pilot, Raymond Baxter, later a well-known BBC commentator, broadcasting as the formation flew over the Royal Review. Once the formation was out of site of the Royal Box I dropped out of it and returned to circle the stadium whilst the broadcast continued. I had been briefed with a minimum height to fly, but Raymond signalled to me to go lower. I did go down a little but the broadcast continued to confirm that we were at the briefed altitude.

Operating a 'foreign' aircraft, parts were often in short supply, and so we were encouraged to fly whenever we could, whatever we could, in order to keep our flying hours up. It was for this reason that one morning I found myself taking part in an in-shore defence exercise, flying an old Auster air-observation (AOP) single-engined monoplane. I took a flight engineer with me, and the irony of having two experienced flight engineers in such a tiny uncomplicated aircraft was not lost on either of us. The exercise involved x-craft midget submarines attempting to break through the Firth of Forth, and our job was to locate and bomb them with aluminium sea markers. We were also told to look out for frogmen who would be coming ashore at first light.

We decided to fly low, very low as it happens, flying the length of the coast so that we could actually see the footprints caused by the frogman coming ashore. Coming in from the sea side along the north shore we happened upon the mighty Forth Bridge right in front of us and did the only thing open to me – we flew under it. Of course there was considerable consternation from some of the navy types seeing us flying so low, but we had been told what to do and as far as I was concerned, we were simply obeying orders. It may have been why my next posting was to an AOP squadron.

I had enjoyed my time on 217 Squadron but it was considered that my work was done. I was posted to Headquarters of 2nd Tactical Air Force on May 15, 1954, and officially to 652 (AOP) Squadron the following day. This AOP was commanded by a major in the Royal Artillery (RA) and comprised five flights, each commanded by a Captain RA. A little after I joined I was delighted to discover that the new commanding officer was to be a Major Cresswell, no less a man than Keith Cresswell's brother with whom I had served on 35 Squadron. It was a happy coincidence.

I was sorry to leave 217 Squadron, and sorry to leave Coastal Command. In many ways it was the pinnacle of my career. As a flight commander it was the first time I had really been in charge, and had more than 150 aircrew and 130 technicians under my command.

I had now served in three commands of the RAF – Bomber, Transport and Coastal – and they were all very different. Coastal Command was especially enjoyable because the captains of the aircraft were given the tactical freedom to operate as they wished. This was not the case with Bomber Command, where we were obliged to follow strict orders, and the actions of others. As a coastal pilot, we tended to hunt alone, and had to be all-round tacticians. If we saw a submarine, it was up to us what happened next, and the approach that we took. Both Coastal Command and Bomber Command were different again from Transport Command, where our sole purpose in life was to keep our passengers happy, and their assets safe!

Now serving with a joint RAF/army observation squadron, we were a part of the British Army on the Rhine (BAOR). I was content stooging up and down the German countryside during the exercise season in a De Havilland Chipmunk with our corporal pay clerk in the back. We would visit the sections where their artillery batteries would be, and where the RA officer pilots would be 'spotting' for our artillery and guiding the ubiquitous 25-pounders onto the target. I was the number two to the CO, responsible for 200 officers and other ranks, as well as around 30 civilians. My career, however, was on the verge of taking another turn, but this time not of my own making.

On January 12, 1956, I was obliged to attend the British Military Hospital in Rinteln, Germany where the army MO picked up on my deafness. In the conversation that followed, I told him that I had been suffering a little for the past year or so, especially after flying. He conducted a few preliminary tests and then referred me to a further ear, nose and throat specialist at the RAF hospital in Wegberg. The squadron leader went through my whole medical history: abscess over left frontal

1936 (*sic*); mumps 1943; jaundice; two attacks of baratrauma with perforated drums – did not report sick. A note also to say 'was doing range work with 25-pounders for a short time last year – never in prolonged contact with noise apart from aero engines. Flying: 3,000 hours in Halifaxes, Lancasters, Wellingtons, Neptunes, Yorks.'

The most damning lines, however, follow soon after: 'F/L Stocker has a severe bilateral conductive deafness. The tympanic membranes are normal and both tympaniums are easily auto-inflated. The rinne is markedly negative. It would seem that a diagnosis of otosclerosis is probable. I think a hearing aid is indicated as he has considerable difficulty at conferences etc. In my opinion he is no longer fit for flying duties and can attain a category no higher than A4G2 in a suitable branch.'

The squadron leader MO wasn't quite done, however, and requested a second opinion from a more senior officer to confirm his verdict. On February 9 I attended the first of what was to be a series of Medical Boards that would determine my fate, and my future career. The first diagnosis of otosclerosis was confirmed, and I was asked to consider proposals of fenestration, a hearing aid and lip reading. I was also given three weeks sick leave in order to arrange new accommodation for my family back in the UK. Our time in Germany was rapidly coming to an end.

I thought about the proposals that had been put to me and signed up both to the idea of lip reading, and having a hearing aid, both of which would require Air Ministry authorisation. I was banned from any branch of the service that required Hearing Standard 1: this included air traffic control, the RAF Regiment and the provost! Within a month I had been fitted with an aid, and made considerable progress in lip reading. I was then instructed to return to my unit, and await AM instructions.

My fate was effectively sealed. I couldn't fly, and if I was to be allowed to stay in the RAF, there was a ceiling both to the opportunities that were open to me, and any further promotions. I might have retired as one of the oldest flight lieutenants the service had ever seen. I was still only 34. The

RAF had been my life, but now I needed to find another. I was formally invalided out of the RAF on September 8, 1956, by which time I had already found employment. The writing had of course been on the wall for some time, and so I had taken it upon myself to contact every aircraft company I could think of, looking for a job. I received a positive response from the De Havilland Engine Company where I was promptly interviewed by a Polish engineer who had been a leading aircraftsman (LAC) in the RAF during the war. I can't remember what I did or said, but it was enough to get me a three month trial on the princely sum of 10 guineas a week (three shillings a day).

I was employed as a trainee weight control engineer spending the first three months at Stag Lane and then a further three months in Hatfield looking at aircraft loading. With my engineering background, I found the job an interesting one. I was responsible for the preparation of aircraft loading data on all new experimental aircraft. That meant advising on weight control specifically in relation to the installation of aero engines – be they piston, gas turbines or rocket motors.

Quite early on during my time at De Havilland I found myself unintentionally on the wrong side of a strike. It so happened that I wasn't part of the union, primarily because I had never been asked to join. When the staff walked out on strike, therefore, I crossed the picket line and they were none too pleased. I decided I needed to enquire further about what the union – the Draughtsmen and Allied Technicians Association (DATA) – stood for, and since I couldn't find a good reason not to belong, I duly became a member. I then proceeded to become more actively involved than perhaps I had originally intended. If somebody is representing me then I like to know a bit more about them.

The union was what we then termed very 'red', and the chairman of the Edgeware branch of DATA was a well-known communist, Ken Gill. I volunteered to become our branch subscriptions secretary, a dogsbody job by any other name, but it meant I was close to what was going on. With the AGM fast approaching, and nominations being sought for the post of branch secretary, I had been canvassing support from a few friends who felt as I did about the reds having it all their own way. One of these friends was Charles Hickling, and Charlie came with me on the night of the vote. The name of Ken's preferred candidate was read out, and the members were asked if there were any objections to his appointment. I duly stuck my arm up and said that he was 'not eligible'. This caused quite a stir, as you can imagine, and so I had to point out that he was not eligible because he was in arrears with his subscriptions!

I thought Ken was going to erupt. Of course the man in question offered to pay straightaway, but I referred to the union rule book that stated that any subscriptions had to be settled afterwards, and could not be made during the meeting. Since he was not eligible, I then nominated Charles as branch secretary (I was always one to lead from the back) and he was duly elected. (As an aside, Ken went on to become the General Secretary of the Amalgamated Union of Engineering Workers and a thorn in the side of the conservatives and New Labour alike; Charles Hickling too rose to high rank in union circles and later played a key role representing trade unions on employment tribunals.)

I spent the better part of two years with De Havilland before in 1959 DHE became part of Bristol Siddeley Engines (BSE) and I had the year before been promoted to be a stress engineer. This meant being responsible for the stress analysis of engine installations and for the supervision of the design of engine transit equipment in line with Ministry of Aviation standards.

The joining of DHE and BSE was a forced marriage by Her Majesty's government. Unfortunately in an engineering environment changing the name on the door does not always work as I found out. A year or more after the amalgamation we were asked to investigate the cause of engine oil leaks, some of which had been blamed for a number of recent crashes. These leaks were at a point where there had not been a problem in several years.

A designer produces his design on plain paper, but when issued for manufacture, the blueprint is on paper which has been pre-printed with the company name and various standards, including manufacturing tolerances. It turned out that there were minor differences between the standards followed by the two companies; normally this did not matter but we were dealing with a banjo bolt. When stressing any item, calculations are made on what can be described as 'minimum possible metal'. When recalculated on the BSE tolerances, the bolt strength was less. I asked the chief inspector to find me a bolt on the most adverse dimensions that was within the new tolerances, and then accurately measure the length. Next I asked one of the experimental fitters to fit it using the correct torque. We then dismantled the bolt, and inspected its length again. As I had suspected, the bolt had stretched. It no longer had the elasticity to maintain an oil tight joint.

One of the aircraft I came across was the Blackburn Buccaneer, a Fleet Air Arm replacement for the Supermarine Scimitar. I worked on one of the original prototypes – I think it was NA39 coded XK488 – for some tests we were carrying out in the summer of 1961. She was the third out of a batch of 20 ordered for the Navy, the last of the three development aircraft in her original markings and colour scheme.

The Buccaneer had a crew of two, the wings folded (so that it could be easily stored on aircraft carriers) and the fuel was all in the fuselage. By my calculations, the aircraft was correctly loaded, and the pilot charged down the length of the runway for take-off. It didn't. Rather than taking to the air, as I expected, the Buccaneer kept going. Fortunately, at the end of the runway was an escape net with a naval anchor chain for just such an eventuality. Unfortunately, the aircraft was travelling so quickly that it went straight into the net and dragging both the net and the chain behind it charged into a greenhouse full of tomatoes. The two crew members emerged shaken, but otherwise unhurt, and I noted that for a few days after the incident I was no longer 'Ted' but 'Mr Stocker'.

Happily, as it transpired, the accident wasn't my fault. We re-checked our loading calculations and nothing was wrong. The Buccaneer had an all-flying tail, so that when the pilot pulled the stick back for take-off, the horizontal part of the tail unit moved. It was important, therefore, that the angle for take-off was set correctly, and to assist the pilot he had an indicator in the cockpit to align the position of the tail. Unfortunately, something wasn't working properly, and so the aircraft would never have been able to get off the ground. (Later they painted angles on the tail.) Three good things came of this incident: firstly, I was vindicated, and my professional integrity was intact; secondly, I went back to being called 'Ted'; and thirdly, there were plenty of tomatoes to go round! The aircraft was back in the air the following year and I believe now resides at the Fleet Air Arm Museum at Yeovilton.

All the time I was at De Havilland and Bristol Siddeley I was also at night school, studying first at Willesden Technical College and later at Hendon College of Technology to further my education. At Willesden I attained an ONC and subsequently endorsements, studying mathematics, applied mathematics, workshop technology, and the principles of electricity. I obtained my HNC at Willesden in the theory of machines, strength of materials and applied thermodynamics, and HNC endorsements at Hendon, studying aircraft structures and industrial administration. I also squeezed in an O level in English Language from the University of London.

My time with Bristol Siddeley came to an end in 1965 when I applied for and was appointed as a piping designer working for Humphreys and Glasgow. I had been bemoaning the state of the aviation industry and Bristol Siddeley in particular where there was little or no chance of promotion or transfer to other parts of the business, and which was forcing many of our engineers to seek employment in Canada and South Africa where their talents were better rewarded. I was at a party with Norman Beck, a friend and fellow engineer who was then working for H&G, and he told me that they were actively recruiting engineers into the petro-chemical industry. I went to their headquarters in Carlisle Place for an interview, and was offered a job and a three months training course. I remember I was also offered the same salary that I was earning at the time, but this time with luncheon vouchers! Three months later and I graduated at the top of the group, and my salary increased accordingly.

The nature of my job, at the time at least, was commercially very sensitive, but basically involved the preparation and use of computer programs to solve issues regarding the design and material selection peculiar to the petro-chemical industry. I had never actually worked with computers before, but was fast becoming an expert in a team that was headed by Henry Spitzer. Our programs were sold to Italian shipbuilders, the national computer centre in Manchester, a Polish shipping company in Gdansk, indeed all over the world.

Although by now I had risen to become chief programmer, I had drifted some distance from my preferred profession as an engineer, although I had been elected to become a member of the Institution of Mechanical Engineers – a membership of which I am still proud – and would later also be entitled to have the letters C.Eng as a chartered engineer after my name.

A meeting with Eric Hill, chief draughtsman at Badgers, then a leading engineering and construction company in the petroleum and chemicals industries, enticed me to leave H&G with the promise of more engineering work, and specifically working on the area of material take-off in piping. I should have known better. Within a week, Eric asked whether I knew much about computing, and the next thing I know I'm flying out to Boston in the US to assess a new program. There was one particularly amusing incident a little later when I was asked to return to the US for a six-week secondment. The idea of being away for such a long time did not really appeal and so I asked if I could take my wife, Pat, and Wendy with me. To begin with they refused, as there was nothing in their company policy that would allow it. The director in charge tried to appeal to my sense of adventure: "Wouldn't you want to go to America on an aeroplane?" he asked. I had much amusement in telling him that not only had I already done so several years before, but I had also flown one back. In the end we agreed an ex gratia payment was sufficient to buy airline tickets for Pat and Wendy to come with me and everyone was happy.

Badgers, part of Raytheon Corporation, decided to reduce its exposure in Europe, and one by one the offices closed (the office in Holland was the last and only one left). By then I had left to go freelance, undertaking a variety of tasks including a project for Ferranti on the north circular. They needed a particular piping and instrumentation diagram, asked if I was available, and asked if I could start that same day. I remember it well because I wanted to have lunch first and start in the

Illuminate someone's worldview
for less this Black Friday

Give the gift of insight with a digital
subscription for $104.50 each year

- Economist app and access to economist.com
- Digital newsletters
- Podcasts and narrated articles
- The digital archive
- Live virtual events

Include our weekly print edition
for $220 each year

See our full range of gift subscription offers online

 Visit: economist.com/G423H

 Call toll free: 1-800-456-6086 and quote code G423

Please allow two weeks for delivery of first issue. Local sales tax, if applicable,
will be added. **Offer valid through November 27th 2023.**

The Econo[ ]

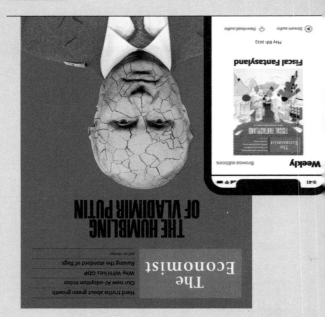

afternoon. This meant I was still working at the time that everyone else wanted to go. I was simply given the keys and told to lock up!

I spent a time working for Foster Wheeler in Reading, another business in the petro-chemical sector in which I was now a specialist. As a project engineer I had responsibility for dealing with a host of different suppliers and contractors installing new pipelines, whilst all the time keeping our bosses and our client happy. I became quite expert in meetings where I learned three valuable lessons: always organise a meeting for late morning to allow all parties ample time to get there; always arrange beer and sandwiches for lunch; always take control of the minutes. I also learned to deal with the various pressure groups and environmental bodies, with obvious concerns about our laying pipes through their beautiful countryside. On one project in the New Forest, animal welfare experts stood by with oxygen containers lest we disturbed a hibernating smooth snake. On the same project, which involved laying pipes from the mainland to Brownsea Island in the middle of Poole Harbour, we had to plug the end of the pipes to prevent the red squirrels from escaping and the grey squirrels from going across.

I officially retired in 1989, although still found I was in demand. I even spent a brief period delivering vehicles for Meon Valley Ford, and when they realised that Pat could drive, they roped her in too!

For the last 20 years I have been kept busy. I was pleased to be a founder member of The Little Staughton Pathfinder Association, attending regular 582 Squadron reunions and spending two years as the association's chairman. I have enjoyed also my time at various Bomber Command events, signing countless books and prints for grateful enthusiasts, and every three years I have been pleased to maintain my links with the modern-day 'Brats' as a member of the Halton Aircraft Apprentice Association. Much of my time is spent helping Pat with her horse, where I always seem to get the dirty jobs. The irony is not lost on me: I started out as a farmer's son working in the fields; and it seems somehow appropriate that I have ended up back in the fields.

As I look back, and I finish writing these words with Sean, we are looking through various scrapbooks and records from my life. I come across a photograph of my time on 35 Squadron, Linton-on-Ouse, September 1941. At the front, I can clearly make out Leonard Cheshire, and 'Pop' Watts standing well to the right, remarkable for his obvious maturing years and the crown above his stripes to denote his flight sergeant status. I am standing at the back. I turn the photograph over and there is a note written on the reverse. It states: 24 flight engineers. 14 dead. Four prisoners of war. Four taken off flying. Two survived.

I am lucky and content with the way my life has turned out. The RAF apprenticeship at Halton gave me a kick-start and the RAF the opportunity to move on. The big regret is that my hearing prevented me continuing as a pilot. My definition of the world's best job is still to be an RAF pilot.

At my age, my memory is not as good as it was. Without the patient and diligent research by Sean in providing the catalyst to revive long half forgotten memories this book would have been a lot shorter and less interesting. I must admit I have enjoyed re-remembering most of the things almost forgotten.

Appendix A

Pilots who flew Ted Stocker

35 Squadron

Pilot	Fate (where known)	Trips shared
F/S Stan Greaves	Shot down 24.7.41	
P/O McGregor-Cheers	Killed in action 25.8.41	
P/O Johnston		
P/O Brown		
F/L Leonard Cheshire	Later VC, OM. 101 ops	
Sgt Williams		4
Sgt Steinhauer RCAF	Killed in action 31.3.42	

102 Squadron

P/O Lashbrook	Shot down 16.4.42	
S/L Griffiths		2
Sgt Boothright		1
Sgt Hank Malkin	Later Group Captain DFC & Bar	23
F/S Barr RCAF	Killed in action 17.6.42	
F/S Wheeler		
W/C Bintley DSO DFC	Killed in flying accident 24.10.42	2
Sgt Newell		
F/S Morgan	Killed in action as P/O 26.6.42	1
F/L Welsh		1
F/S Duff RCAF	Killed in action 26.6.42	
F/L Hamilton		1
F/S Kent		
F/L Debenham		
S/L John Walkington	Killed in action 3.12.42	
S/L Robinson		1
P/O Drummond		
F/S Towse		

35 Squadron (Graveley)

P/O MacKenzie		
S/L Peter Elliott DFC	Killed in action 2.3.43	
S/L Franklin		
F/L Paxton		2
W/C Basil Robinson DSO DFC AFC	Killed in action 24.8.43	2
P/O George Herbert	Killed in action 12.6.43	2
F/S Quigly	Shot down in action 21.6.43	3
P/O Robert Appleby	Killed in action as F/L DFC 5.1.44	
S/L Keith Cresswell	Later DSO DFC	
W/C 'Dixie' Dean DSO DFC		1
F/S Daniel		

F/S Matich DFM RNZAF	Shot down and evaded 27.9.43. Later DSO	
F/L Julian Sale	DSO & Bar, DFC Died of wounds 20.3.44	
F/L Davidson DFC		
F/L Wood		1
Air Commodore Bennett CBE DSO	Later Air Vice-Marshal CB	
F/L Roache		
P/O Danny Everett	Later DFC & 2 Bars KIA 8.3.45	
W/C Pat Daniels	DSO DFC & Bar	
F/O Ken Price		
F/L Webber		
S/L Wesser/F/L Jones		

7 Squadron Oakington

S/L Campling DSO DFC	Killed in action 15.2.44	
W/C Tatnall OBE	Killed in action 15.2.44	
F/O David Davies	Posted to 582 sqdn	30

582 Squadron Little Staughton

F/L 'Bill' Spooner	Later DFC & Bar	2
F/L John Goddard DFC	Killed in action 8.9.44	1
W/C Peter Cribb DSO DFC	Later Air Commodore and Bar to DSO	7
F/L Freddie Gipson DFC		1
F/L Godfrey O'Donovan	Later DSO DFC	2
F/L Clyde Magee		1
F/L Reg Hockly DFM		1
F/L Walter Reif	Killed in action 23.12.44	1
F/L Paddy Finlay	Later DFC & Bar	2
F/L Richard Berney DFM	Later AFC	2
F/L Jimmy Brown	Later DFC & Bar	2
F/O Hal Mettam		1
S/L Kenneth Swann DFC		1
F/L Harte-Lovelace DFC		3
S/L Vivian Owen-Jones DFC		
F/L Martyn Nairn	Later AFC	1
P/O Oswald Interiano	Later DFC	
W/C Stafford Coulson DFC	Later Group Captain DSO	
F/L Arthur Macaulay	Later DFC	
S/L Norman Mingard	Later DSO DFC	
S/L Gavin Brownell DFC	Later Bar to DFC	
S/L Cairns DFC		

The authors would welcome any further information on any of the pilots listed above, and their fates.

Appendix B
Operational record of Flight Lieutenant Edward Stocker DSO DFC

35 Squadron – Linton-on-Ouse – Halifax

Op	Pilot	Target	Date	Time	Notes
1	Sgt Williams	Essen	11.10.41	6.20	
2	Sgt Williams	Nuremberg	12.10.41	8.25	a/c crash landed
3	Sgt Williams	Bremen	21.10.41	4.50	
4	Sgt Williams	Hamburg	26.10.41	6.25	

102 Squadron – Dalton/Topcliffe – Halifax

5	W/C Bintley	Le Havre	14.4.42	6.00	
6	S/L Griffiths	Lorient	16.4.42	7.20	
7	F/S Morgan	Dunkirk	24.4.42	4.00	
8	S/L Griffiths	Kiel	28.4.42	6.30	
9	F/L Welsh	Paris	30.5.42	5.25	
--	F/L Welsh	Essen	1.6.42	DNCO	Pilot's ears u/s
10	F/S Malkin	Essen	5.6.42	5.40	
11	W/O Malkin	Osnabrück	19.6.42	4.20	
--	W/C Bintley	Bremen	25.6.42	1.20	Returned on three engines
12	F/L Hamilton	Bremen	27.6.42	5.05	
13	W/C Bintley	Bremen	29.6.42	5.30	One petrol tank holed
14	F/S Boothright	Düsseldorf	31.7.42	4.40	Landed Swinderby
15	S/L Robinson	Osnabrück	10.8.42	4.50	

35 Squadron – Graveley – Halifax

16	P/O Malkin	Karlsruhe	2.9.42	6.30	Landed Wyton. PFF sortie
17	P/O Malkin	Bremen	4.9.42	5.20	
18	P/O Malkin	Duisberg	7.9.42	4.10	
19	P/O Malkin	Frankfurt	8.9.42	4.20	Shot up by e/a over Luxemberg. Lost one engine. Captain wounded
20	P/O Malkin	Aachen	5.10.42	5.45	Flew as MUG
21	W/C Robinson	Milan	24.10.42	8.45	
22	P/O Malkin	Hamburg	9.11.42	3.00	Thick smoke from bomb bay at 4° 15' E. Dropped flares and bombs
23	P/O Malkin	Turin	18.11.42	7.25	Landed Tangmere
24	P/O Malkin	Lorient	14.1.43	5.00	PO feathered on return. PI cut on landing
25	P/O Malkin	Lorient	15.1.43	4.20	
26	P/O Malkin	Berlin	16.1.43	7.40	Returned on three engines
27	P/O Malkin	Lorient	23.1.43	4.40	
28	F/O Malkin	Lorient	16.2.43	4.15	Malkin promoted F/O
29	F/O Malkin	Wilhelmshafen	19.2.43	4.40	

30	F/L Malkin	Nuremberg	25.2.43	7.05	Malkin promoted F/L
31	F/L Malkin	Cologne	26.2.43	4.25	One engine u/s
32	F/L Malkin	Berlin	1.3.43	7.50	Lost PI engine and rudder on target. Restarted. Lost PO engine later. Coned for 25 minutes. MUG wounded. Landed Swanton Morley
33	F/L Malkin	Essen	5.3.43	4.05	
34	F/L Malkin	Nuremberg	8.3.43	7.40	
35	F/L Malkin	Munich	9.3.43	7.40	
36	F/L Malkin	Essen	12.3.43	4.00	
37	F/L Malkin	Lorient	2.4.43	4.55	
38	G/C Robinson	Frankfurt	10.4.43	5.50	
39	F/L Paxton	Pilsen	16.4.43	8.45	
40	F/L Paxton	Stettin	20.4.43	9.15	
41	P/O Herbert	Düsseldorf	25.5.43	5.15	
42	P/O Herbert	Essen	27.5.43	5.00	
43	F/S Quigly	Munster	11.6.43	4.50	
44	F/S Quigly	Bochum	12.6.43	4.40	
45	F/S Quigly	Le Creusot	19.6.43	6.10	Returned at zero ft. Shot up train and flak ship
46	W/C Dean	Mannheim	9.8.43	5.40	
—	F/S Daniel	Milan	12.8.43	3.00	DNCO PO u/s on French coast
47	F/L Wood	Hannover	27.9.43	4.50	
—	F/O Price		29.12.43	3.10	Hydraulics u/s. U/c and flaps would not come up. Bombs dropped 20mins after take-off from 30/40ft

7 Squadron – Oakington – Lancasters

48	F/O Davies	Leipzig	19.2.44	7.15	First time as b/a
49	F/O Davies	Stuttgart	21.2.44	6.00	
50	F/O Davies	Schweinfurt	24.2.44	7.00	
51	F/O Davies	Augsburg	25.2.44	7.35	
52	F/O Davies	Stuttgart	1.3.44	7.20	
53	F/O Davies	Stuttgart	15.3.44	7.15	
54	F/O Davies	Frankfurt	22.3.44	5.30	
55	F/O Davies	Berlin	24.3.44	7.15	Returned on three engines

582 Squadron – Little Staughton – Lancasters

56	F/O Davies	Aachen	12.4.44	3.45	
57	F/O Davies	Noissy-Le-Sec	18.4.44	4.35	
58	F/O Davies	Cologne	20.4.44	4.10	
59	F/O Davies	Laon	22.4.44	4.05	
--	F/O Davies	Karlsruhe	24.4.44	2.30	DNCO PO u/s
60	F/O Davies	Essen	26.4.44	4.35	
61	F/O Davies	Aulnoye	28.4.44	3.10	
62	F/O Davies	Somain	30.4.44	3.00	
63	F/O Davies	Nantes	7.5.44	4.40	
64	F/O Davies	Louvain	11.5.44	3.00	
65	F/O Davies	Dortmund	22.5.44	4.05	
66	F/L Davies	Aachen	24.5.44	4.15	Davies promoted F/L
67	F/L Davies	Fôret de Cerisy	7.6.44	3.25	

68	F/L Davies	Laval	10.6.44	4.15	Master bomber
69	F/L Davies	Lens	15.6.44	2.45	Returned on three engines
70	F/L Davies	Coutrolle	24.6.44	2.10	
71	F/L Davies	Blainville	28.6.44	5.20	Deputy master bomber
72	F/L Davies	Villers Bocage	30.6.44	2.20	
73	F/L Davies/ F/L Grant	St Philiberte	14.7.44	2.35	DNCO. Heavy Oboe
74	F/L Davies	Nucourt	15.7.44	3.15	
75	F/L Davies	Caen (North)	18.7.44	3.00	
76	F/L Davies	Mount Candon	19.7.44	2.35	
77	F/L Davies	Lisieux	22.7.44	3.05	Nav two slightly wounded by flak
78	F/L Spooner	Bremen	18.8.44	5.15	
79	F/L Goddard	Stettin	29.8.44	9.20	
80	W/C Cribb	Le Havre	5.9.44	2.35	Master bomber
81	W/C Cribb	Le Havre	6.9.44	2.00	Master bomber
82	F/L Gipson	Le Havre	8.9.44	2.25	Backer up
83	G/C Cribb	The Hague (V2)	17.9.44	2.30	Master bomber
84	S/L Spooner	Cap Gris Nez	26.9.44	2.20	Deputy master bomber
85	F/L O'Donovan	Calais	28.9.44	2.30	Master bomber
86	G/C Cribb	Westkapelle	3.10.44	4.10	Master bomber
87	G/C Cribb	Wanne Eickel	12.10.44	3.50	Master bomber
88	F/L Magee	Wilhelmshafen	15.10.44	4.35	
89	F/L Hockly	Düsseldorf	2.11.44	4.15	
90	G/C Cribb	Julich	16.11.44	3.50	
91	F/L Reif	Heimbach	3.12.44	3.45	DNCO. Weather
92	S/L O'Donovan	Hannover	5.1.45	5.00	
93	F/L Brown	Wiesbaden	2.2.45	5.05	
94	F/L Finlay	Cologne	2.3.45	4.20	
95	F/L Finlay	Hemmingstedt	7.3.45	6.00	
96	F/L Nairn	Dortmund	12.3.45	4.35	
97	F/L Berney	Dülmen	22.3.45	4.00	
98	F/L Berney	Paderborn	27.3.45	5.30	
99	F/L Brown	Lutzkendorf	4.4.45	7.15	
100	F/O Mettam	Kiel	9.4.45	5.30	
101	G/C Cribb	Berchtesgaden	25.4.45	7.00	
102	S/L Swann	Rotterdam	1.5.45	2.50	Manna
103	F/L Harte-Lovelace	Juvincourt	8.5.45	4.35	Exodus
104	F/L Harte-Lovelace	Lübeck	10.5.45	3.00	Exodus
105	F/L Harte-Lovelace	Juvincourt	15.5.45	1.30	Exodus/ Petrol tank u/s

Acknowledgements

Of course the first person I should like to thank is Ted himself. I enjoyed my many trips down the A3 on the way to or from clients, and the occasional pint and a sandwich shared with Pat and Wendy. What a gang, and what a great privilege it has been to work with them all in getting Ted's story down on paper.

My thanks in particular to Francis Hanford, head curator at The Trenchard Museum, RAF Halton, and to the founder and archivist Min Larkin for their warm welcome, strong coffee and sound advice. They could not do enough to help, including putting me in touch with Air Chief Marshal Sir Michael Armitage to write the foreword. He did both Ted and me a great honour.

My thanks also to the many whose small contributions added up to a large amount of useful material, including Ron Fulton at Boscombe Down, Bill Hough for his contemporary account of Arthur Harris' tour of Brazil, Clive Harte-Lovelace, Leslie Zwingli and Stephen Rees for details of their respective fathers' wartime careers, and Dave Wallace.

Of particular assistance with photography I would like to thank Alex Goldberg of the Flight Collection (Image Asset Management, Birmingham, 0121 744 0433) for permission to reproduce the splendid 'Portraits from the famous Pathfinder Group' pages from a 1945 issue of *Flight*. My friends at the Pathfinder Museum at RAF Wyton, especially Johnny and Sharon, were also most supportive, and I look forward to working with them, Jim and Andy on future projects.

Special mention should go to the Grub Street team for the work that they do in ensuring stories like these are recorded for history, and produce – in my opinion – the finest quality books in the world of aviation. I was a collector long before I became an author.

As usual, my work colleagues Iona, Alex and Alison listened with patience as Ted's story came together, and probably now know as much about Ted's life as I do. Given that this is the third book completed since Iona has been at the company, I now expect her to be an expert on Bomber Command!

Finally my thanks to the genius that is my wife, Elaine, and the boys Matt and James who probably think that their dad is no longer 'kl' (apparently that's MSN-speak). Lol.

Sean Feast

Index

NOTES

NOTES